CLEAN
&LEAN DIET
COOKBOOK

OVER 100 DELICIOUS
HEALTHY RECIPES WITH
A 14-DAY MENU PLAN

James Duigan, world-renowned wellness guru and
co-owner of Bodyism, London's premier health and
wellness facility, is one of the world's top personal trainers.
His glittering client list includes Elle Macpherson,
Rosie Huntington-Whiteley and Hugh Grant.

KYLE BOOKS

CLEAN & LEAN DIET
COOKBOOK

OVER 100 DELICIOUS HEALTHY RECIPES WITH A 14-DAY MENU PLAN

JAMES DUIGAN

with Maria Lally

PHOTOGRAPHY BY
SEBASTIAN ROOS AND
CHARLIE RICHARDS

KYLE BOOKS

First published in Great Britain in 2012 by

Kyle Books

23 Howland Street

London W1T 4AY

general.enquiries@kylebooks.com

www.kylebooks.com

ISBN 978 0 8578 300 74

Text © 2012 by James Duigan and Maria Lally

Recipes by Clara Grace Paul @ www.claracooks.com

Design © 2012 by Kyle Books

Location photographs © 2012 by Sebastian Roos

Holly Valance photograph (page 7) Lickerishltd.com/ Huggy Ragnarsson

Elle Macpherson photograph (page 30) © James Houston/ Corbis Outline

Recipe and food photographs © 2012 by Charlie Richards except for pages 24-25 and 56 by Will Heap, page 54 Martin Brigdale, page 154 Yuki Sugiura and page 158 Catherine Gratwicke

Editor Judith Hannam

Design Dale Walker

Model Christiane Duigan

Clothes by Grace and Favour at b.PR

Recipe home economy and styling Emma Jane Frost

Copy editor Anne Newman

Proofreader Anna Irvin

Production Nic Jones, David Hearn and Lisa Pinnell

A Cataloguing in Publication record for this title is available from the British Library.

Printed in China

Disclaimer

The information and advice contained in this book are intended as a general guide. Neither the author nor the publishers can be held responsible for claims arising from the inappropriate use of any remedy or exercise regime. Do not attempt self-diagnosis or self-treatment for serious or long-term conditions before consulting a medical professional or qualified practitioner. Do not begin any exercise programme or undertake any self-treatment while taking other prescribed drugs or receiving therapy without first seeking professional guidance. Always seek medical advice if any symptoms persist.

CONTENTS

by Holly Valance

Ask me to do something, and I probably won't. Ask me not to, and I'll hop to it! It's always been that way! So when James and I started out on our first training session I figured I had another bloke who'd turn out to be Chief Sarge of the Fun Police and poo poo everything I've always done, and try to make me do things I've never really been interested in doing to begin with. Guess what? I was wrong. Which I've only been once before, obviously.

~

Becoming Clean & Lean is the simplest, most enjoyable lifestyle choice I've made, and the only one I've actually stuck to. And it's been easy. Clean & Lean eating is common sense, and your body doesn't have to go through any torturous reactions – as it does with silly fads – to get results.

~

My training sessions are really enjoyable. My body has responded how I always wanted it to, but never did before. With Clean & Lean James has really tapped into how we can function at the highest levels realistic to our busy lifestyles. That's why you'll get results. And that's why you'll stick to it. It really is that easy.

~

You need to be healthy first and foremost. Inside and out. And the hardest part is actually your head. Once you decide you want to be at your optimum, whatever that may be for you, focus on that, and not on what the Barbie girl who's been retouched within an inch of her life looks like.

~

So, remember:

We can't all be supermodels. We can all be Clean & Lean. There's an opportunity through exercise and diet to create a longer healthier life, a calmer mind and better existence for ourselves. And that's what this is really about. Living life better!

CHAPTER 1

INTRODUCTION

THIS CHAPTER WILL REVEAL:

1. WHY YOU NEED TO BE CLEAN TO BE LEAN

2. THE EXCUSES THAT ARE STOPPING YOU FROM BECOMING SLIM AND HEALTHY

3. HOW OUR COVER GIRL GOT HER BODY

'Thousands of people have changed their lives by becoming Clean & Lean. It's a term I came up with to describe the perfect body: 'Clean' of fattening toxins and 'lean' and healthy as a result. No more excuses. NOW is the time to change your life'

AN INTRODUCTION FROM JAMES

Since writing *Clean & Lean* and *Flat Tummy Fast*, my wife, Christiane and I have been overwhelmed by the inspirational stories we have read from people whose health, bodies and lives have been transformed by the books. So the first thing I want to say to the thousands of you all over the world who have shared your beautiful stories and asked me for more Clean & Lean recipes is: thank you. It is because of you that I have written this book.

I love food! Christiane and I start talking about lunch before we finish breakfast, and my happiest moments are when I am eating good food with family and friends. But I also understand that we all have a complicated relationship with food, and often, our behaviours are driven by things that happened in our childhood – trauma, abuse, self-punishment and scarcity, to name a few. Let me share a little bit of my own story with you now, in the hope that it might help somebody.

I grew up in quite a poor home where, sometimes, there was no food on the table. Other times, there wasn't even a table. There was, however, lots of love, laughter and singing and, no matter how bad things were, my dad was a super-hero and always made things OK. So I feel very lucky to have had the things I had, but being hungry sucked. It is an enduring and powerful memory from my childhood and it affected my relationship with food for years without me ever knowing. I never understood why I ate the way I did – why I would binge eat until I felt sick and could hardly move. And, regardless of what I'd already eaten, I could never leave anything on my plate. I guess all this came from a deep belief that food was scarce and that I didn't know where my next meal was coming from. Now that I understand what was driving this behaviour, I can tell the hungry little glutton inside me that there is plenty of food and that I don't need to eat everything I see. Recognising this has helped me to deal with it, and I hope this may get some of you thinking about any of your own eating habits that aren't working for you and why they happen in the first place.

One of my other enduring memories is of my mother's beautiful cooking. She could make anything taste great and she instilled in me a deep appreciation for good food cooked well. We grew a lot of our own vegetables and she always tried to get organic food whenever she could in whichever town or city we were living in at the time. She also noticed that whenever I had sugar I would throw a tantrum and run around in circles for twenty minutes, then cry for an hour (that still happens to this day), so my childhood was largely sugar-free, apart from the epic binges I managed at grandparents' and friends' houses. Although at the time being the only sugar-free kid didn't feel so good, I'm grateful for it now, as I feel it has played a big part in me feeling so healthy as an adult. My relationship with food is now one of unconditional love: I love food and food loves me.

So this is not a diet book. Many books about getting in shape are anti-food, but this one is different. I want to help you change your relationship with food and see it as something to be enjoyed while you're relaxed and happy, not something that stirs up feelings of shame, guilt and despair, leaving you feeling miserable and helpless. I want you to love food, and to find as much joy in it as Christiane and I do.

Food is one of our main life sources. It nourishes us, keeps us strong and can make us look and feel amazing. It lifts our mood and our energy levels. When you view it in this way, and eat nourishing foods that are good for you, the weight will drop off and you'll feel amazing. But when you view food as the enemy, as something that is 'bad' for you, you'll remain stuck in that all-too-common cycle of deprivation and 'reward' – the reward being a binge on fatty, sugary foods that gives you a quick, fleeting high followed by a feeling of sickness, tiredness, and, ultimately, guilt and shame. Then the cycle of deprivation will start all over again.

This book features some of my own favourite recipes, and I've asked some of my friends – including Elle Macpherson, Rosie Huntingon-Whiteley and Hugh Grant – plus my brilliant team at Bodyism to share with you some of theirs too.

I also talk about the attitudes of other cultures towards food. I've travelled extensively and have picked up tips on what works from countries all over the world. In Australia, for example, where I come from, eating is a very sociable activity; we love our meat and vegetables, and enjoy BBQs and eating outside. You can follow the Clean & Lean rules wherever you go and still enjoy your food, if you take note of what I say in the following chapters. Plus, there are delicious recipes from all over the world for you to try.

A VERY QUICK REMINDER ABOUT THE CLEAN & LEAN REGIME

A body can never be lean unless it's clean. That's the first principle, and it's toxins, which are stored in the fat cells, that you need to avoid. If you're dieting, but toxic, your body will lose fat, but the toxins will have nowhere to go other than back into your system. This is why you often soon feel terrible after starting a diet – tired, lethargic and headachey. Your body quickly decides it doesn't like feeling this way and therefore holds on to fat in order to store toxins, and so the cycle continues. If you're toxic, you'll always struggle to lose weight and, ironically, many diets make you more toxic with all their low-fat/high-sugar advice. However, if you stick to 'clean' foods that are toxin-free, unprocessed and close to their natural state, you'll lose weight easily and keep it off.

WHAT ARE CLEAN FOODS?

✳ They haven't changed much from their natural state. For example, that apple in your fruit bowl looks like it did when it was hanging on the tree, yet crisps don't resemble potatoes. That's because they've been processed.
✳ They don't have any added artificial flavour.
✳ They don't last for months on the shelf. Clean foods develop mould or go off quite quickly because they're natural and not packed with life-lengthening preservatives.
✳ They don't have long lists of ingredients, many of which you can't even pronounce, let alone recognise.
✳ They don't list sugar among their first three ingredients – sugars usually end in 'ose', e.g. fructose, sucrose, glucose.

WHAT ARE THE CLEAN & LEAN RULES?

Here's a quick run through of the rules.

SUGAR – NOT SO SWEET

Sugar makes you fat. It converts to fat quicker than fat itself because it raises your insulin levels, which causes fat storage. Studies show that 40 per cent of the sugar you eat is converted straight to fat, and that's in a slim person. If you're already overweight, up to 60 per cent is converted straight to fat and stored around your stomach, waist and hips. Put simply – if you eat sugar every day, you'll always struggle to lose weight.

Sugar also leaches vitamins from your body, and a body starved of vitamins is a hungry one. That's one of the main reasons that overweight people are always hungry – they don't eat enough vitamin-rich food and are malnourished. It also makes you tired and weakens your immune system. Lots of so-called 'diet' or 'low-fat' foods and drinks are packed with sugar because, yes, it is technically low in fat, but the sugar converts to fat.

ANOTHER KEY CLEAN & LEAN RULE IS TO CUT OUT CRAP

Cut the CRAP* (that's *Caffeine, Refined sugar, Alcohol and Processed foods) ©
Caffeine is OK in small doses. One or two cups of coffee a day won't do much harm. Some studies suggest it can even help with fat burning, especially if you drink the organic kind. Green tea also contains caffeine and you can have up to six cups of this a day (any more will affect your sleep). The trouble with too much coffee (which contains more caffeine than green tea) is that it puts stress on your system. When we're stressed, we release a hormone called cortisol which encourages our body to cling to fat. So to sum up, one or two coffees = fine; too many = a fat middle.

I've already talked about refined sugar – in cakes, biscuits, 'diet' foods and drinks, chocolate and fizzy drinks – so let's move on to alcohol now. Alcohol is full of sugar and, as a result, it makes you fat around the middle. It also stimulates the production of the hormone oestrogen, which promotes fat storage around your waist and tummy. Remember, too, that the liver is a fat-burning organ so when it's processing alcohol, it stops burning fat. In short, alcohol leaves you squidgy around the middle.

Processed foods go against every Clean & Lean rule there is. The less a food has been altered, the 'cleaner' it is, which is good news for our waistlines. Clean foods are very close to – if not the same as – their natural state. Processed foods, on the other hand, are usually made in factories, stripped of their natural goodness and pumped full of man-made preservatives and additives to make them look appetising and last longer. So stay away from bread, pasta and white rice, some tinned foods, ready meals, most breakfast cereals and frozen chips and wedges.

FAT DOESN'T MAKE YOU FAT

Don't be fat phobic! When I talk about fat, I mean good fat – the heart-friendly kind found in nuts, avocados, oily fish and oils, not bad fat, on the edge of a strip of bacon or other processed meat, or in a pie crust. Good, clean fats should be eaten every day. They encourage your body to burn fat around your middle, and to absorb vitamins and minerals more efficiently. Good fats also reduce sugar cravings, lift your energy levels and ability to concentrate and keep you full for a long time.

WHERE ARE TOXINS FOUND?

Toxins are found in the following:
* Sugar
* Alcohol
* Fizzy drinks
* Processed foods
* Processed 'diet' foods
* Excess caffeine
* Artificial sweeteners
* Food additives
* Preservatives
* Artificial colour
* Artificial enhancers, like MSG and many E numbers e.g. E621 is a sneaky way of saying MSG
* Pesticides – wash your fruit and veg thoroughly

WHAT'S YOUR FOOD HANGOVER?

Food can make you feel really, really good. I'm talking energised, alert, slim, fit and young. It can make your skin glow and your hair shine. But food can also make you feel really, really bad too. If you eat the wrong types of food, it can make you feel fat, bloated, tired and guilty. So think about how you want to feel before you next eat.

You see, I don't actually believe that overweight or unhealthy people enjoy their food. Sure, I think they like the look of that chocolate bar, or the smell of fish and chips, but how do they feel after eating it? Pretty bad. I know, because that's what my clients tell me when they speak about their past battles with food. You need to decide whether you want food to make you feel good or bad? It's a simple choice, and I think we both already know the answer, otherwise you wouldn't have picked up this book.

If you do struggle with food, bingeing or yo-yo dieting, try turning your negative thoughts into positive ones. A very effective strategy for changing your negative habits to positive ones that transform your body and life is to say affirmations and practise visualisation. So for example:
Don't think: 'I'm fat, I look disgusting and feel bloated.'
Think instead: 'I am so slim, healthy and feel beautiful. Weight loss is effortless and easy.'
Don't think: 'I can't have that chocolate bar,' or, if you just ate a chocolate bar, 'I feel guilty for eating that.'
Think instead: 'I listen to my body and nourish it with only the foods that make me feel amazing and energised. I am safe and all is good.'
Don't think: 'I haven't got time to make a healthy meal or exercise.'
Think instead: 'I love and care for my body. Abundance of time and health flows to me.'
Or try visualisation: at any time of day or when you are drifting off to sleep or waking up, picture your legs, tummy, bum, arms – your whole body – looking the way you want it to look, and emphasise the sense of how that makes you feel. Do this as regularly as you remember.

So change your thoughts and beliefs and you can instantly change your emotional state.

'Eating is my favourite thing to do!'

Our cover girl – and Mrs James Duigan – Christiane, reveals why changing her relationship with food changed her body:

Since I met James in 2006 I've discovered just how much I love food. James and I love to eat – it's one of our favourite things to do! Whenever we travel abroad we rate the country on the food we eat there and love discovering new dishes and restaurants. In fact, we're such foodies our friends are always asking us for recommendations on where to eat.

Before I met James, I had a very different relationship with food. I ate less than I do now and exercised more. Now I know that I was eating all the wrong types of food for my body like fruit, low-fat yogurts, had only salad on a plate and drank skimmed milk and diet drinks. I was hungry a lot of the time – but heavier. I often felt guilty when I did eat fatty foods, so I would wolf them down, but then feel even worse afterwards. And so the cycle would continue...

Then I met James and he told me about Clean & Lean. No food was off limits, but I had to listen to my body and let it be my own personal nutritionist. So if a food made me feel tired, heavy, windy or bloated, I avoided it. If I wanted some lasagne or pasta, I'd have it, but I'd eat it slowly and savour every mouthful. I wouldn't feel guilty – I would enjoy it but, crucially, I would stop when I was full or starting to feel uncomfortable. By just enjoying the food

and feeling good about what I was eating, the weight fell off and I haven't gained a pound since.

The key to being slim is to enjoy your food. Any transformation that happens in the body, happens in your mind first. What you are thinking and feeling will be reflected in your body. You have to try it to believe it!

James, we all can't thank you enough. Hundreds of people have written in after reading your books to express their gratitude to you for the transformation and impact you have made on their lives. You have inspired so many people to make positive changes to their health, bodies and lifestyle. You have always wanted to make a difference in the world and help others and you have done that through your persistent kindness, love and generosity. From your family, friends, clients and everyone that has read your books – THANK YOU!

On a personal note, Amor, not only have you changed my life in terms of health you have brought me so much love and happiness. I have found a love with you like no other and I am so grateful for you, our friendship and to have you as my husband. My happiest moments are with you, creating our amazing life together since the moment we fell in love over chocolate soup! You're a true inspiration and I'm so proud of you. Thank you, Te amo muito!!.

A FINAL WORD

When I was publicising my first two books, I met lots of readers. One woman was overweight and miserable as a result, but tried to tell me she was 'too busy' to do anything about it. She said she didn't have time to prepare her meals. 'Fine,' I told her. 'Just have some pre-cooked chicken or salmon and salad or something easy like an omelette with greens when you get in from work.' But she said she didn't have time. When I suggested she try to walk for thirty minutes a day, or try a yoga class every now and then, she told me she didn't have time for that either. She was negative and wanted to prove to me she didn't have time to look and feel good. She had kids and a busy job, she kept saying. Then another woman – who was slim and healthy

looking – said to the two of us: 'I've got three kids too, and a job, and a house to run. But I make time to eat the right stuff and move around a bit when I get the chance.' This encounter made me realise that some people look for obstacles when it comes to getting in shape. Instead of thinking you can't do it, know that you can. You just have to decide whether you want to look and feel slim and healthy or you don't. It's a choice, and only you can make it.

This book is a celebration of food. So read and enjoy all the tasty recipes I've put together here for you. I want you to have fun, to feel good and to share that with the people you love. Let me know what you think!

CHAPTER 2

CLEAN AND LEAN MENU PLANS

THIS CHAPTER WILL REVEAL:

1. YOUR PICK 'N' MIX MEAL PLANNER

2. THE 14-DAY MENU PLAN

YOUR PICK 'N' MIX MEAL PLANNER

To prove just how easy the Clean & Lean diet is, I've devised a Pick 'n' Mix chart. It contains three lists of different foods (protein, vegetables and 'flavour') plus a list of cooking methods. All you need to do is pick your favourite protein, your favourite vegetables, favourite flavour and cook it using your preferred cooking method.

Guide...

1 With your protein, just pick one and have an amount roughly the size of the palm of your hand or a deck of playing cards.

2 With the vegetables, feel free to pick as many different types – and as much – as you like.

3 Feel free to add a small handful of nuts and/or beans or lentils to your meal. It will fill you up and help prevent those snack cravings sneaking up on you later.

A NOTE FOR VEGETARIANS

If you're a vegetarian, feel free to substitute the proteins I've suggested for your usual non-meat source (for example, eggs, beans, lentils, tofu etc). As for cheese, go for hard white cheeses such as feta and goat's cheese. Avoid the heavily processed cheeses that are bright yellow or come in slices and go for the best quality, organic cheese you can afford.

PROTEIN

* Any fish
* Chicken
* Turkey
* Prawns
* Veal
* Lamb
* Beef
* Duck
* Eggs
* Avocado

VEGETABLES

* Broccoli
* Kale
* Spinach
* Green beans
* Asparagus
* Rocket
* Cucumber
* Courgette
* Leeks
* Peas
* Pak choi
* Beetroot
* Peppers
* Sweet potato
* Aubergine
* Carrots
* Mushrooms

FLAVOUR

* Olive oil
* Flax oil
* Garlic
* Herbs, fresh and dry
* Mustard seeds
* Lemons
* Limes
* Chilli
* Ginger
* Camomile
* Passionflower

HOW TO COOK

* Grill
* Bake
* Steam
* Sauté
* Stir-fry
* Barbecue
* Blanch

TRY TO AVOID

* Frying
* Boiling
* Microwaving

THE 14-DAY EATING PLAN

When you feel ready to start, follow this 14-day plan. It's best to start on a weekend, when you have more time on your hands to get everything ready. Plus you won't feel so stressed or rushed, which will mean you'll be less likely to supplement the plan with a quick coffee or a mid-afternoon chocolate bar.

You can swap meals around (have Day 1 breakfast on Day 2, for example), but try to stick to the plan as much as possible. You shouldn't feel hungry, but if you do, just increase your green vegetable portions and make sure you're drinking enough water (at least 2–3 litres of still, filtered water a day).

Where possible (and if you can afford it), go for organic ingredients – especially when it comes to eggs (free-range are also good) and meat.

DAY 1

Breakfast: Omelette, with your choice of ingredients from the list on p. 42

Snack, mid-morning: 100g chicken breast and ¼ avocado

Lunch: Elle's kale and goat's cheese salad (p. 60)

Snack, mid-afternoon: 2 hard-boiled eggs and ½ cucumber, sliced

Dinner: Seared sirloin with rocket and watercress salad (p. 96)

DAY 2

Breakfast: Perfect porridge with berries, yogurt and almonds (p. 38)

Snack, mid-morning: 100g turkey and 5 walnuts

Lunch: Quiche with brown rice crust (p. 67) – a great lunch option as it can be made the night before and eaten cold

Snack, mid-afternoon: 100g sliced salmon with ¼ avocado

Dinner: Seared wasabi and sesame tuna with chilli green beans (p. 96)

WHAT IS A 100G

If you don't have scales to weigh your portions, here's a rough guide to the measurements given in the 14-day plan below:

100g chicken = two thirds the size of a regular breast or the palm of your hand (minus fingers)

100g smoked salmon = the size of your outstretched hand

100g beef fillet = the size of a tennis ball

DAY 3

Breakfast: Green smoothie (p. 169)

Snack, mid-morning: 100g salmon and 6 pecan nuts

Lunch: Crunchy Cambodian-style beef salad (p. 70) – again, another great recipe to eat cold for lunch

Snack, mid-afternoon: 100g cooked prawns with ½ yellow pepper

Dinner: Grilled cajun chicken (p. 99)

DAY 4

Breakfast: Poached eggs with asparagus and smoked salmon (p. 41)

Snack, mid-morning: 100g chicken breast and 12 cashew nuts

Lunch: Clean & Lean wrap (p. 73)

Snack, mid-afternoon: 100g turkey slices with ½ green pepper, sliced

Dinner: Lamb cutlets with chermoula dip and roast courgettes (p. 105)

DAY 5

Breakfast: Elle's quick scrambled eggs (p. 59)

Snack, mid morning: 100g turkey slices with 5 hazelnuts

Lunch: Green super salad (p. 69)

Snack, mid-afternoon: 100g beef slices and ¼ cucumber, sliced

Dinner: Whole baked sea bass (p. 92)

DAY 6

Breakfast: Deliciously flaked granola (p. 35)

Snack, mid-morning: 100g sliced chicken breast with ½ red pepper, sliced

Lunch: Red and yellow salad with mackerel (p. 68)

Snack, mid-afternoon: 100g chicken breast and ½ sliced tomato

Dinner: Grilled chicken or turkey with radicchio salad (p. 88)

*top tip

Poaching doesn't require any oil or fat and the result is a succulent, tender chicken

DAY 7	DAY 8	DAY 9	DAY 10
Breakfast: Buckwheat pancakes (p. 32)	**Breakfast:** Scrambled eggs, smoked salmon & asparagus (p. 45)	**Breakfast:** Goat's cheese and egg white omelette (p. 42)	**Breakfast:** Morning booster smoothie (p. 167)
Snack, mid-morning: 100g chicken breast and 6 pecan nuts	**Snack, mid-morning:** 100g salmon with ½ red pepper, sliced	**Snack, mid-morning:** 100g turkey breast and ¼ avocado	**Snack, mid-morning:** 100g chicken breast and 12 cashew nuts
Lunch: Hugh's cold lamb salad (p. 68)	**Lunch:** Clean & lean lettuce wrap (p. 73)	**Lunch:** Green super salad with grilled chicken (p. 69)	**Lunch:** Clean & lean lettuce wrap with chicken, tomato and avocado (p. 73)
Snack, mid-afternoon: 100g chicken breast and ½ sliced tomato	**Snack, mid-afternoon:** 100g turkey with a portion of steamed green beans	**Snack, mid-afternoon:** 100g turkey with ¼ cucumber, sliced	**Snack, mid-afternoon:** 100g chicken breast with ½ yellow pepper
Dinner: Rosie's roast chicken (p. 106)	**Dinner:** Turkey burgers (p. 106)	**Dinner:** Balinese steamed fish (p. 118)	**Dinner:** Lamb steak with mushy peas (p. 102)

*it's easy

Good healthy habits are a choice and once they are part of your lifestyle they will last you a lifetime

DAY 11	DAY 12	DAY 13	DAY 14
Breakfast: Poached eggs with spinach and mushrooms (p. 41)	**Breakfast:** Turkey with avocado, goat's cheese and tomato	**Breakfast:** Scrambled eggs with prawns and spinach (p. 59)	**Breakfast:** Deliciously Flaked granola (p. 35)
Snack, mid-morning: 100g turkey and 4 macadamia nuts	**Snack, mid-morning:** 100g beef slices and 5 walnuts	**Snack, mid morning:** 100g chicken slices with 5 hazelnuts	**Snack, mid-morning:** 100g turkey with 5 Brazil nuts
Lunch: Hugh's cold lamb salad (p. 68)	**Lunch:** Beluga Salad (p. 64)	**Lunch:** Gazpacho (p. 55)	**Lunch:** Clean & lean lettuce wrap (p. 73)
Snack, mid-afternoon: 100g salmon with ½ green pepper, sliced	**Snack, mid-afternoon:** 100g sliced turkey breast with ¼ avocado	**Snack, mid-afternoon:** 2 hard-boiled eggs and ½ cucumber, sliced	**Snack, mid-afternoon:** 100g turkey breast and ¼ cucumber, sliced
Dinner: Chicken skewers (p. 74)	**Dinner:** Grilled chicken or turkey with radicchio salad (p. 88)	**Dinner:** Grilled cajun chicken (p. 99)	**Dinner:** French Nicoise salad (p. 131)

*top tip
Stick this plan on your fridge as a constant reminder, then you won't be tempted to stray

CHAPTER 3

CLEAN AND LEAN BREAKFASTS

THIS CHAPTER WILL REVEAL:

1. WHY CEREAL MAKES YOU FAT

2. HOW ELLE MACPHERSON STAYS HEALTHY

3. QUICK, DELICIOUS RECIPES YOU CAN MAKE IN MINUTES

One of the most important parts of the Clean & Lean regime is to have a good breakfast. What you eat for breakfast determines how your body deals with fat for the whole day, so it's very important to get this meal right. The right breakfast will lift your mood and energy levels and will turn your body into a fat-burning machine for the rest of the day. But if you get it wrong, you'll crave sugar all day and your energy levels and mood will sink fast.

My perfect breakfast is some clean and lean protein in the form of organic fish, eggs, chicken or even some steak. I cook it the night before and have it cold in the morning with some green beans or broccoli. This leaves me feeling bulletproof. Chicken and green beans for breakfast? Yes, it sounds crazy but once you get your head around it, you'll realise it's the best thing you can have.

Marketing people have programmed us into picking one of two options for breakfast – two slices of toast with a processed topping or a bowl of sugary cereal with little goodness. Possibly a fry-up or scrambled eggs (which are great by the way) as a treat.

But cereal is just about the worst breakfast imaginable. It's over-processed, often full of sugar and contains zero protein, except possibly the milk. The sugary ones aimed at kids are the worst, but the so-called healthy ones aren't much better. Porridge is the only one that's good – have it with nuts, seeds and berries and you've got a great little breakfast. But as for the rest? Avoid them.

If you – or your children – have cereal in the morning I guarantee you'll be hungry and tired by midday, looking for something sugary to snack on to lift your flagging energy levels. Protein keeps you full, so cereal for breakfast is like putting water in your car instead of petrol. It will fool you for a little while into thinking you've eaten, but you'll be hungry very quickly afterwards and will have to snack throughout the day.

Protein and greens, on the other hand, are the perfect combination for breakfast. The protein – be it chicken, fish, eggs – will keep you full for hours and will fire up your metabolism; the greens will provide a hit of vitamins and fibre, which will improve your overall health and wellbeing. It may take a while getting used to having this sort of thing for breakfast, but just try it for a week and see how amazing you feel. If you're not keen on chicken first thing, eggs and smoked salmon have always been a popular choice for breakfast, or have a couple of scrambled eggs with half a sliced avocado. After a while, try out other 'protein and green' combinations, like chicken and avocado, smoked salmon with green beans or – my favourite – steak with broccoli.

THE CLEAN & LEAN BREAKFAST RULES

Here are my breakfast rules:

1 Include protein and greens in your breakfast if you can. But at the very least, you must have some protein in the morning – be it eggs, smoked salmon, meat, cheese, milk or yogurt.

2 Eat within an hour of waking up to really get your metabolism fired up. If you leave it any longer your body slips into starvation mode and so clings to fat. Eating within an hour of getting up breaks your fast (hence the name), and your body cranks up its fat-burning abilities ready for the day ahead.

3 Take Bodyism BodyBrilliance every morning – a fat-burning blend of antioxidants. Mix two teaspoons with water and have it with your breakfast. Available at www.bodyism.com.

Drink up – how to hydrate at breakfast

In a perfect world, I'd suggest you have some slightly cooled boiled water with a squeeze of fresh lemon juice when you first wake up. It's the perfect drink to hydrate you and detox your system. If you can get into this very quick and simple habit, you'll notice a difference in your energy levels, skin and hair, and you'll look less bloated. Another good option is a cup of green tea. But at the very least you should be drinking a glass of water as soon as you wake up. Have one by your bed and sip it as you get up.

Coffee or tea in the morning is fine. Everyone loves it and I certainly wouldn't advise you not to have it, but have one of the options above first. Just stick to one cup of coffee or tea at breakfast (leaving you free to have another mid-morning or lunchtime). Buy a good-quality, organic coffee or tea and have it with organic full-fat milk, which is better for you than skimmed. If you're eating Clean & Lean overall, you don't need to worry about the extra calories in full-fat milk. I always take it – or even organic cream – in my coffee and I'm slim. Full-fat milk contains more calcium and will keep you fuller for longer. Plus, good natural fats won't make you fat, if the rest of your diet is clean.

Green tea is also great to have every morning. It also contains caffeine, but less so than coffee and many more antioxidants. You can drink up to six cups a day and I tell all my clients to drink it.

HOW I STAY HEALTHY – BY ELLE MACPHERSON

I've known James for nearly twenty years and I still use his Clean & Lean philosophy to this day. When we started working together he immediately understood that I wanted to maintain a long, lean, healthy body whilst retaining my femininity and curves. But he also understood that I'm a busy woman – especially after having my two sons – trying to fit in healthy eating with a demanding job and two children. I just don't have the headspace to be obsessive at the gym or about food.

What works for me is his balanced approach, which results in a healthy, vibrant and strong body. I choose to forgo quick fixes, drastic regimes and hours pounding my body in the gym. All I need is the right information and the motivation to do what's required.

As I've got older my body, and metabolism, have

changed – what worked for me in my 20s and 30s doesn't work for me now. But as always, James and I have worked together to find a solution; nutritional tweaks, along with amazing stress-relieving and body-energising supplements. James' approach is non-gimmicky and straightforward. He works from the inside out and I'm in the best shape ever because of this.

We're both Australian and we love an outdoor lifestyle and the same kinds of food. A true testament to James is we're still working together after all these years. Why? Because he keeps things relevant and fun – it works! There is literally nobody better in the world than James for getting a woman's body into amazing shape. After all, check out his wife in this book! She's a true testament to the Clean & Lean way of life.'

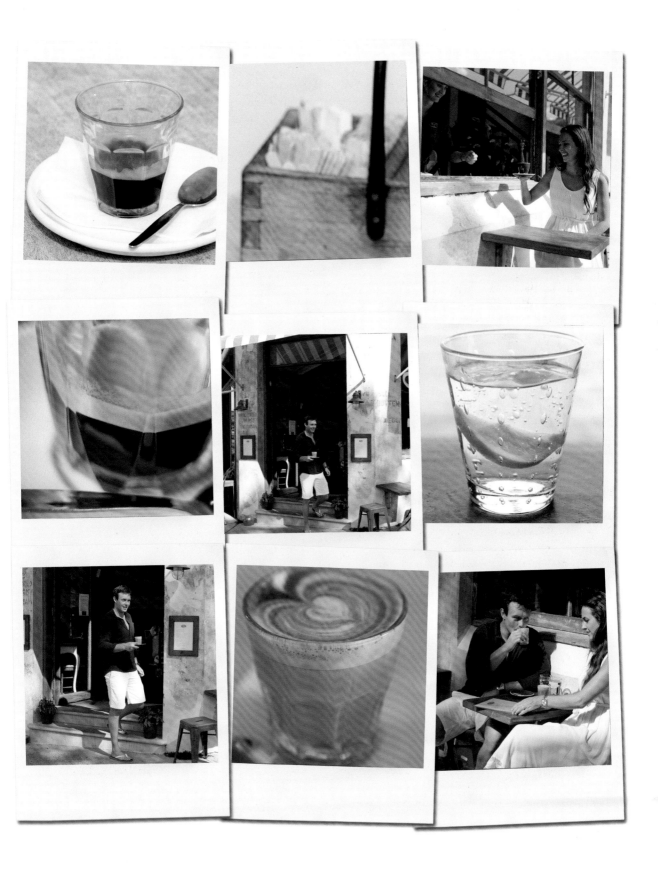

*top tip

Berries are rich in antioxidants to detox your system, packed with vitamin C which helps your body deal with stress, and full of fibre which helps to regulate blood-sugar levels

Clean & Lean Oat Pancakes

Serves 2-4

Ingredients
100g rolled oats
200g fat-free cottage cheese
4 eggs
1 teaspoon cinnamon

Method
1. Blend the ingredients in a food processor.
2. Pour a ladleful into a heated pan and cook for 2-3 minutes on each side.

My top breakfasts

My absolute perfect breakfast is sitting in the sun at a café called **Trio** at Bondi Beach, eating boss eggs (the best eggs in the world, they have feta cheese and truffle oil in them) with my beautiful family and my beautiful, gorgeous wife. We sit there and we laugh and listen to the great music the owner plays. **Kensington Square Kitchen** in London does incredible eggs and coffee; and **Gjelina's** in Los Angeles do an incredible wholemeal, organic egg sandwich with the yummiest coffee in the West Coast. Then there is **Norma's** in New York that does epic breakfasts that last till lunch time.

Buckwheat and Blueberry Pancakes

Serves 4

Ingredients
275ml milk
1 large organic egg
55g wholemeal flour
55g buckwheat flour
150g blueberries
vegetable oil, for frying
maple syrup, for drizzling

Method
1. In a large bowl, whisk the milk and egg together, then gradually add the flours and whisk well until you have a smooth batter. Stir in the blueberries.

2. In a heavy-based frying pan, heat 1 teaspoon oil. Once hot, spoon in a small ladleful of the batter and keep in a small round shape.

3. After 2-3 minutes, flip and cook for the same amount of time. Repeat until you have roughly 8 pancakes.

Toasted Pecan and Oat Blueberry Crunch

Serves 4

Ingredients

200g pecans, chopped
100g walnuts, halved
100g desiccated coconut
200g rolled oats
1 teaspoon ground cinnamon
150g blueberries
organic natural yogurt, to serve

Method

1. Preheat the oven to 180°C/350°F/gas mark 4.

2. In large bowl, mix together the nuts, coconut, rolled oats and cinnamon. Spread on to a baking sheet and toast in the preheated oven for roughly 10 minutes, or until golden, turning halfway through cooking.

3. Leave to cool, then toss with the blueberries and serve with the yogurt.

*top tip

Swap the walnuts for almonds or pistachios if you want, or combine a delicious mixture of all three

*top tip

You can use any grain you like in this; I often choose a mixture of quinoa flakes and oats

Deliciously Flaked Granola

Ingredients

550g rolled oats
4 tablespoons coconut oil
2 tablespoons ground cinnamon
3 teaspoons vanilla seeds
35g sunflower and pumpkin seeds
2 tablespoons linseed or flaxseed
30g pecan nuts, broken in to small pieces
30g cashews or any nut of your choice
1½ tablespoons toasted or dried coconut

Method

1. Preheat the oven to 190°C/375°F/gas mark 5 and line two baking trays with parchment paper.

2. Put the oats, 2 tablespoons coconut oil, cinnamon and vanilla seeds in a bowl and mix well. Spread the mixture evenly on to the prepared baking trays, then place in the preheated oven. Bake for 20 minutes, checking throughout and tuning after 10 minutes.

3. Heat 2 tablespoons coconut oil in a pan and add the seeds, nuts and coconut. Lightly toast until slightly golden, then set aside to cool.

4. When everything is cooled, mix together and place in a glass jar or storage container. Then this is ready for you to have as a healthy breakfast with some organic natural yogurt, to use as a topping for crumbles or to add some crunch to some berries. Enjoy!

Gluten-free Sprouted Bread with Smoked Salmon and Avocado

Serves 4

Ingredients
4 slices gluten-free sprouted grain bread
200g smoked salmon
2 avocados, halved and sliced
black pepper
1 lemon, quartered

Method
1. Preheat the grill.

2. Warm the bread slices under the preheated grill and serve with the smoked salmon, avocado slices, black pepper and lemon wedges.

Mackerel with Rye Bread

Serves 1

Ingredients
1 mackerel fillet
50g cottage cheese
juice of ½ lemon
sea salt and freshly ground black pepper, to taste
a slice of rye bread

Method
Mix the mackerel, cottage cheese, lemon and salt and pepper together and serve on rye bread. This is also great as a snack.

*top tip
If you don't have any time to make breakfast, just grab half an avocado, slice it up and have it on a few oatcakes

*top tip

You can prepare this awesome source of essential fatty acids beforehand and keep refrigerated in a plastic container

Super Oatmeal

Serves 2

Ingredients
1 apple
3-4 apricots
280ml water
150g rolled oats
200g unsweetened mixed berries, fresh or frozen
10 cardamom pods
20g flaxseeds
20g hemp seeds
1 teaspoon cinnamon
40g sunflower seeds
40g pumpkin seeds
40g raisins

Method
1. Grate the apple, chop the apricots and mix in a pan with the water, oats and half of the berries. Bring to the boil.

2. While the berry mixture is boiling, remove the cardamom from its pods, chop or grind finely and add to the pan. Boil for 10-15 minutes or until the oats are soft and most of the water has been absorbed or has evaporated, then remove from the heat and set aside to cool a little.

3. Place the flaxseeds and hemp seeds together in a blender and blend thoroughly.

4. Stir the flax and hemp seeds into the cooled berry mixture, adding plenty of cinnamon.

5. Serve with the remaining fresh berries, sunflower and pumpkin seeds and raisins.

Perfect Porridge

Serves 1

Ingredients
250ml water/milk/rice milk/almond milk
35g rolled oats
½ teaspoon ground cinnamon
½ teaspoon orange zest
1 teaspoon toasted flaked almonds

Method
1. Place your liquid of choice in a pan with the oats, ground cinnamon and orange zest and bring to the boil, then simmer steadily for a further 5 minutes, stirring regularly.

2. Serve in a bowl with almonds sprinkled on top.

*serving suggestion

Serve with mixed berries and some greek yogurt

Asparagus helps
debloat your
tummy, making
it a great
pre-bikini food

Hugh Grant's
Poached Eggs with Asparagus and Parmesan
Serves 4

Ingredients
2 bunches of asparagus
sea salt and freshly ground black pepper
olive oil, for drizzling
4 fresh organic eggs
Parmesan, for sprinkling

Method

1. Bring a pan of water to the boil and preheat the grill to hot.

2. Place the asparagus on a baking tray, season with salt and pepper and drizzle with olive oil. Grill for approximately 10 minutes, until cooked.

3. Bring a pan of water to the boil, stir rapidly to create a whirlpool and crack the first egg into the centre; the swirling water should bring the egg together. Repeat with the remaining eggs; 3-4 minutes is sufficient cooking time.

4. Serve each egg with asparagus spears and grate a little Parmesan over the top.

Poached Eggs with Ham and Spinach
Serves 4

Ingredients
4 organic eggs
4 slices smoked ham
30g baby spinach

Method

1. Bring a pan of water to the boil, stir rapidly to create a whirlpool and crack the first egg into the centre; the swirling water should bring the egg together. Repeat with the remaining eggs; 3-4 minutes is sufficient cooking time.

2. Serve each slice of ham with a poached egg on top and spinach on the side.

*remember
Always try to buy organic eggs, or free-range at a push, but never battery eggs. Organic eggs have more fat-burning, health-boosting omega-3s and they taste better too

Chorizo Frittata

Serves 1

Ingredients
1 teaspoon olive oil
5 slices chorizo
1 spring onion, chopped
2 organic eggs
20g goat's cheese

Method
1. Put the oil in a pan on a low heat with the chorizo and spring onion and cook for 2 minutes.

2. Meanwhile, whisk the eggs in a bowl, then pour over the ingredients in the pan. Once cooked through, sprinkle the goat's cheese over the top and serve.

Goat's Cheese and Egg White Omelette

Serves 4

Ingredients
3 organic egg yolks
100g soft goat's cheese
sea salt and freshly ground black pepper
5 organic egg whites
1 teaspoon olive oil

Method
1. In a small bowl, beat the egg yolks, goat's cheese, salt and pepper.

2. In a large bowl or food-processor, whisk the egg whites and then fold in the goat's cheese mixture.

3. In a frying pan, heat the oil and, once hot, pour in the omelette mixture. Cook for 2 minutes, loosening the sides with a palette knife or spatula, then fold over one half and continue cooking for a further 2–3 minutes.

*serving suggestion

Add wilted spinach, roast tomatoes, grilled pancetta, chicken, asparagus, courgettes, chillies, turkey, olives, feta, crab or prawns to the omelette before folding in half

Try to eat some avocado every week. It keeps you full for hours, helps your body burn fat and improves the condition of your hair, skin and nails

Grilled Figs with Avocado and Natural Yogurt

Serves 4

Ingredients

4 fresh figs, cut into quarters
2 ripe avocados, halved and sliced
200ml natural yogurt
4 tablespoons shelled pistachios,
lightly toasted and chopped

Method

1. Preheat the grill to high.

2. Place the figs on a baking tray and grill until golden.

3. Serve with the sliced avocado, then spoon over the yogurt and, finally, sprinkle over the toasted pistachio nuts.

*it's easy

If your mornings are rushed, you don't have to grill figs – just have them fresh from the fridge

*note

Don't have eggs every day. It's good to include a wide range of protein in your diet

Scrambled Eggs with Smoked Salmon and Roast Asparagus

Serves 4

Ingredients

a bunch of asparagus, trimmed
2 teaspoons olive oil
sea salt and freshly ground black pepper
8 organic eggs
200g smoked salmon

Method

1. Preheat the oven to 200°C/400°F/gas mark 6.

2. Lay the asparagus on a sheet of foil, drizzle with 1 teaspoon of the olive oil and season with salt and pepper. Bring the corners of the foil together to make a sealed parcel and roast in the preheated oven for 8–10 minutes, until the spears are tender.

3. Meanwhile, in a large bowl, beat the eggs with salt and pepper.

4. Heat the remaining olive oil in a frying pan over medium heat, then scramble the eggs, using a fork to break them up until cooked to your liking.

5. Serve with the smoked salmon and asparagus.

HERE'S MY HANDY 'BAD, BETTER & BEST'

BAD	BETTER	BEST
Bad: Breakfast cereal **Why?** Processed and full of salt and sugar	**Better:** Oatmeal made with milk and fresh berries **Why?** Oatmeal is a slow-release carbohydrate with lots of fibre	**Best:** Oatmeal made with organic milk, fresh berries, nuts and seeds **Why?** The nuts and seeds add healthy fats, which boosts the metabolism and keeps you fuller for longer
Bad: White toast with jam **Why?** This combination of sugar + sugar will leave you sluggish and hungry well before lunch	**Better:** Wholemeal bread with fresh fruit **Why?** These have more fibre than white bread and jam	**Best:** Dark rye crispbreads with organic nut butter **Why?** This is the perfect blend of slow- release energy carbs and fats
Bad: Fruit juice concentrate **Why?** Sugar with little nutritional value	**Better:** Freshly squeezed juice **Why?** Full of vitamins (but still high in fructose/sugar)	**Best:** A freshly squeezed juice made from cucumber, spinach and kale **Why?** Sugar-free, alkalising, nutrient-dense... drink lots of it
Bad: Waffles/pancakes **Why?** Full of sugar and processed flour	**Better:** Gluten-free bread **Why?** No harmful allergens	**Best:** Clean & lean oat pancakes **Why?** A great source of low-GI carbohydrates
Bad: English fry-up: bacon, eggs, sausages and chips **Why?** Very high in saturated fat and salt	**Better:** Poached eggs, grilled bacon and sausages **Why?** Grilling food helps to reduce the saturated fat content of a meal by 25 per cent	**Best:** Soft-boiled eggs, grilled organic sausages and steamed kale or spinach **Why?** Kale is a superfood and organic sausages are rusk- and nitrate-free
Bad: Scrambled eggs and fried bread **Why?** Loaded with saturated fat	**Better:** Scrambled eggs with baked beans **Why?** Beans have fibre, but just make sure you get the low-salt version	**Best:** Scrambled eggs with steamed spinach **Why?** High in Vitamin A and iron
Bad: Tinned fruit **Why?** Full of sugar (from the syrup) and very low in nutrients	**Better:** Mixed fresh fruit salad **Why?** Contains more vitamins and minerals when fresh	**Best:** Fresh berries with natural yogurt and cinnamon **Why?** A perfect blend of carbs and protein

BREAKFAST GUIDE:

BAD	BETTER	BEST
Bad: Ready-to-eat fruit/crunch yogurts **Why?** Sugar dressed up to be healthy	**Better:** Organic yogurt with fruit compôte **Why?** Organic yogurt is better but the fruit inside the pot is still very high in sugar	**Best:** Organic full-fat yogurt with blueberries and mixed nuts **Why?** The perfect blend of protein, fats, carbohydrates, vitamins and minerals
Bad: Muffin **Why?** Full of sugar, wheat and flour	**Better:** Gluten-free muffin **Why?** No harmful allergens but still high in sugar	**Best:** Omelette with organic eggs **Why?** Organic eggs are the healthiest source of protein – the gold standard!

*case study

One of my clients used to skip breakfast and power through the morning on coffee. By lunchtime she was starving, so she would eat whatever she could grab quickly that provided quick-release energy, like a sandwich or a bowl of pasta. After she ate it, she would get the inevitable crash in blood-sugar levels (caused by the spike in energy from all those carbs) and would then have to prop her flagging energy levels up with chocolate or something sweet. She just couldn't lose weight because of all those carbs and sugar.

When she came to see me, the first thing I insisted was that she overhaul her breakfast. I still let her have her beloved coffee, but only one or two cups, max. And I only allowed her to have it once she'd eaten breakfast, not before. For breakfast, she had some lovely lean protein, like smoked salmon or eggs, with something green like avocado and a couple of oatcakes. After the first day, she reported fewer sugar cravings, less hunger and better energy levels all day. By making over her breakfast, the rest of her diet fell into place and she found she could stick to the Clean & Lean regime easily and the weight fell off. But she could only do this once she'd sorted out her bad breakfast habits.

*case study

Another example of a 'bad breakfaster' is a friend of mine. She always had sugar-based breakfasts and wondered why she couldn't shift that half stone she wanted to get rid of, and why she was tired all the time (and we all know that tiredness leads to sugar cravings). When she came to me for advice, I asked her what she had for breakfast. She told me: 'A croissant or some cereal with skimmed milk, if I'm being good.' Good? Cereal with skimmed milk is a terrible breakfast, lacking in protein and bursting with sugar. You must, must have protein with your breakfast, if you want to stay full until lunch, and a bit of skimmed milk just doesn't cut it. As for the croissant, that's another sugar bomb. I told her to ditch the cereal altogether and have some scrambled eggs on rye bread or an omelette filled with greens. If she was busy and didn't have time to make anything, I suggested some full-fat Greek-style yogurt with berries and some oatcakes for a breakfast on the go, or smoked salmon with some avocado. Straight away, she noticed her energy levels were better and her sugar cravings reduced. Thanks to a better breakfast, she stopped snacking on sugar throughout the day and dropped that half a stone in less than a month.

CHAPTER 4

CLEAN AND LEAN LUNCHES

THIS CHAPTER WILL REVEAL:

1. WHY YOU NEED TO DITCH SANDWICHES
2. HOW TO GET THE PERFECT LUNCH, WHEREVER YOU ARE
3. HOW YOU CAN MAKE TASTY LUNCHES IN MINUTES

*it's easy
Visit your local
greengrocers or
farmer's market –
the fruit is nearly
always fresh and
sourced locally

Lunch is another important meal to get right. It needs to keep you going for the rest of the day, so if you get it wrong – or skip it altogether – you're likely to binge when it comes to dinnertime or you'll spend all afternoon snacking on sugary junk food. This affects your quality of sleep (sugar is a stimulant and chocolate contains caffeine) which slows down fat burning further.

Sadly, for many people, lunch is just something processed, containing barely any protein, grabbed on the go and eaten quickly, before getting back to work, or eaten in front of a computer. Many of my clients have busy jobs in the city or are busy mums, and admit to me that they rarely have time for a proper lunch break. Their lunch usually consists of a pre-packed sandwich, followed by (yet another) coffee. The result? They're hungry by 3pm and desperate for something sweet to keep them going until dinner time.

A pre-packed sandwich isn't a good lunch. Take the type you find in the shops – a few slices of (non-organic) chicken, swimming in mayonnaise and squashed between two slices of processed, salty bread with maybe a few measly limp lettuce leaves and tomato slices. How can that keep you going until dinner? Your lunch needs to contain a decent amount of clean and lean protein – a palm-sized amount, ideally. Tiny bits of meat or fish, the amount you find in your average sandwich, just aren't enough. You also need a large portion of brightly coloured vegetables, full of vitamins and minerals that keep you full.

THIS IS WHAT EVERY LUNCH SHOULD CONTAIN:

✳ protein (chicken, fish, eggs, quinoa, tempeh etc.)
✳ fat (the clean and lean kind, such as half an avocado, a small handful of nuts and seeds or a good drizzle of olive or coconut oil)
✳ vegetables (include some that are green, such as lettuce, cucumber and broccoli and some that are brightly coloured, such as tomatoes and peppers).

If I ever have a bad lunch, I feel terrible all afternoon – tired and craving sugar – because I haven't nourished my body properly. So I always try to have a Clean and Lean lunch. My favourite is a salmon and kale salad, which keeps me full and avoids that awful afternoon slump. Wherever I am in the world, I opt for a variation of this – I might swap the salmon for cod, or the kale for green beans or salad.

*remember
Take at least a 20 minute break for your lunch and really savour it. If you 'stress eat', you don't chew thoroughly and your body won't absorb the nutrients efficiently. Concentrate on your food, not your work, so your body registers you are eating and signals when you are full

COOKING THE CLEAN & LEAN WAY – A QUICK REMINDER

The cleanest ways to cook are:

✳ **Steaming** This is one of the healthiest ways to cook fish, meat and vegetables. It retains nearly all the nutrients (and flavour) found in food and doesn't add any fat. As the name suggests, the food doesn't come into contact with the water – just the steam that the water lets off. The most common way to do this is to suspend the food over boiling water, using a steamer (this usually has holes in it to allow the steam through).

✳ **Blanching** This is a way of cooking vegetables that keeps them crisp and tender, but also retains lots of the nutrients. You boil them for a short amount of time, so that they're barely cooked, but still tender. Then you remove them from the heat, drain and add them to a bowl of icy water. Wait until they're no longer warm, then quickly reheat them (by boiling, steaming or grilling for 30 seconds to a minute).

✳ **Grilling** This is a great way to cook meats and fish. Lots of the fat drips away, plus it gives a lovely flavour to your food.

✳ **Baking/roasting** There isn't any real difference between these two. They're both methods of cooking meat, fish and vegetables using dry heat (your oven), which browns the food's exterior and cooks the middle.

And the worst ways to cook are:

✳ **Frying** Usually, this involves cooking foods with oil in a hot pan. Firstly, the oil soaks into the food and secondly, because that fat is heated up, it becomes less healthy (cold olive oil is far healthier than hot olive oil).

✳ **Boiling** When you boil vegetables they lose many of their health-boosting nutrients. Blanching is OK because you're only boiling them for a short amount of time, but when you just boil your vegetables for a long time, you'll lose too many nutrients.

✳ **Microwaving** It may save you time, but microwaving your food is one of the worst ways to cook. Some studies show it destroys 97 per cent of the health-boosting antioxidants found in vegetables.

*it's easy
Save time and don't cook vegetables – you won't lose nutrients that way!

*note
Cold olive oil is much healthier than when it is heated, and it also tastes better too

Clean & Lean Minestrone

Serves 4

Ingredients

150g haricot beans
1 tablespoon chopped sage
1 onion
1 leek
1 celery stick
1 courgette
¼ red pepper
½ aubergine
200g spinach
200g white cabbage
2 tablespoons olive oil
1 garlic clove, finely chopped
a sprig of thyme
1 small tomato, finely diced
500ml organic vegetable stock
100ml tomato juice
a generous pinch of sea salt and freshly ground black pepper
grated Parmesan, to garnish

Method

1. Soak the beans in water overnight to soften.

2. Dice the onion, leeks, celery, courgette, red pepper and aubergine, ensuring they're cut the same size.

3. Slice the spinach and cabbage into fine strips.

4. Heat the oil in a large saucepan and add the onions, leeks, celery and garlic and fry until soft. Add the rest of the vegetables and cook for a few minutes further.

5. Add the thyme, beans and tomato and fry for a further 5 minutes. Add the vegetable stock and tomato juice, bring to the boil and cook until the vegetables are soft.

6. Lastly, add the cabbage and spinach, season with salt and pepper and add the grated Parmesan when ready to serve.

*top tip

Soup is great because it hydrates you and keeps you full for hours. Make it in big batches and keep it in the fridge or freezer for a quick and easy meal

Gazpacho

Serves 2

Ingredients
700ml fresh tomato juice
4 tablespoons extra virgin olive oil
2 large ripe tomatoes, chopped
1 cucumber, chopped
1 small onion, chopped
1 red pepper, deseeded and chopped

Method
Place the ingredients in a blender and
whizz for 1 minute.

Squash, Ginger and Sesame Soup

Serves 4

Ingredients

2 tablespoons sesame oil
1 onion, chopped
2 celery sticks, sliced
2 carrots, peeled and chopped
2 garlic cloves, chopped
1 x 5cm piece of fresh ginger, peeled and finely chopped
a bunch of coriander, roots and leaves separated and chopped
1 butternut or acorn squash, peeled and cut into chunks
1 litre organic vegetable or chicken stock
sea salt and freshly ground black pepper
2 tablespoons sesame seeds, lightly toasted

Method

1. Heat the oil in a large pan over a medium heat, then add the onion, celery, carrots, garlic, ginger and coriander roots and cook for 10 minutes.

2. Add the squash and cook for a further 10 minutes, or until it begins to soften.

3. Add the stock and salt and pepper, bring to the boil and simmer for roughly 20-25 minutes, until the squash is cooked.

4. Place the soup in a blender and whizz until smooth. Adjust the seasoning and serve topped with the toasted sesame seeds.

Spinach, Pea and Tarragon Soup

Serves 4

Ingredients

2 tablespoons olive oil
1 onion, chopped
1 leek, thinly sliced
2 garlic cloves, chopped
a bunch of tarragon
250g baby spinach
1 litre organic vegetable or chicken stock
sea salt and freshly ground black pepper
500g petit pois
juice of ½ lemon
extra virgin olive oil, for drizzling

Method

1. In a large pan, heat the oil and gently fry the onion, leek and garlic until softened, approximately 10 minutes.

2. Add the tarragon and spinach, and once the leaves are wilted, add the stock and salt and pepper. Bring to the boil and add half the peas. Cook for a further 5 minutes, then remove from the heat.

3. Place the soup in a blender and whizz until smooth, then add the lemon juice and the remaining peas. Adjust the seasoning if necessary before serving with a drizzle of extra virgin olive oil.

Broad Bean Dip
Serves 4

Ingredients
400g broad beans, fresh or frozen,
podded weight
200ml organic natural yogurt
juice of 1 lemon
1 garlic clove, crushed
sea salt and freshly ground black pepper
4 tablespoons extra virgin olive oil
a small bunch of mint, very finely chopped
1 tablespoon tahini paste

Method
1. Blanch the beans in a pan of boiling salted water for 4 minutes. Drain and run under cold water.

2. Place the beans in a blender with all the other ingredients and whizz until smooth. Taste for seasoning and adjust if necessary.

Guacamole
Serves 4

Ingredients
2 ripe avocados
1 medium tomato
juice of ½ lemon
½ red onion
sea salt, to taste

Method
Place all the ingredients in a blender and whizz for 20 seconds or until desired consistency is reached.

Spinach and Artichoke Dip
Serves 4

Ingredients
a large handful of spinach
50g tinned artichoke
20g grated Parmesan
1 garlic clove
squeeze of lemon juice
110ml soured cream
dill and parsley (about 100g each), to taste

Method
1. Preheat the oven to 180°C/350°F/gas mark 4.

2. Place all the ingredients in a blender and whizz for approximately 30 seconds. Pour into an ovenproof container and bake in the preheated oven for 20 minutes.

Mackerel Kedgeree

Serves 4

Ingredients

1 tablespoon olive oil
1 onion, finely chopped
1 teaspoon ground coriander
1 teaspoon curry powder
275g brown rice, cooked and drained
100g peas
4 naturally smoked mackerel fillets, flesh flaked off the bone
sea salt and freshly ground black pepper
2 hard-boiled organic eggs, peeled and quartered, to garnish

Method

1. In a large frying pan, heat the oil and gently fry the onion, until soft and translucent.

2. Add the ground coriander and curry powder and continue frying for a further 2–3 minutes. Stir in the rice, the peas and the fish. Cook over a low heat, stirring continuously.

3. Serve garnished with the eggs and season to taste.

This is a firm favourite – it takes about 3 minutes and is full of nutrients and minerals. Couldn't be easier or quicker! It's good for a snack any time of day and great for kids as well; and you can throw in any leftovers you may have in the fridge as well to really mix up the brilliant scramble
Elle Macpherson

Elle's Quick Scrambled Eggs

Serves 1

Ingredients

2 organic eggs
generous pinch of sea salt and freshly ground black pepper
splash of milk
½ tablespoon unsalted butter
1 spring onion
a pinch of capsicum

Method

1. Break the eggs into a bowl, season and whisk together with a splash of milk.

2. Heat the butter in a saucepan until it is melted and then add the egg mixture, stirring all the time until they are scrambled and cooked to your liking.

3. Turn the eggs out onto a plate, scatter the onions over the top and add a sprinkling of capsicum to taste.

*top tip

I've had this salad several times and it's yummy. It's great because it's bursting with flavour and so complete – meaning it contains good fat, from the avocado, oil, goat's cheese and seeds, and vitamins from the kale and other vegetables. Kale is also one of the most alkaline foods, which means it reduces inflammation in the body and boosts your immune system

Spring Onion, Watercress and Tarragon Frittata

Serves 4

Ingredients
1½ tablespoons olive oil
a bunch of spring onions, trimmed and sliced, using the majority of the green leaves
2 garlic cloves, crushed
a bunch of tarragon
a bunch of watercress, leaves and thin stalks picked off
8 organic eggs
sea salt and freshly ground black pepper
½ tablespoon olive oil

Method
1. In a small frying pan, heat the oil and over a medium heat cook the spring onions and garlic and tarragon until softened. Add the watercress and continue cooking until wilted.

2. In a mixing bowl, whisk the eggs and add the salt and pepper. Add the spring onion mix and combine well.

3. In a small frying pan, heat the olive oil and add the frittata mix. Over a medium-low heat, cook the frittata, pulling in the edges with a spatula. Meanwhile, heat the grill to medium. After roughly 8 minutes, once the frittata is cooked on the bottom, place the pan under the grill and cook for another 8-10 minutes, until golden and cooked.

4. Enjoy with a green salad.

Elle's Kale and Goat's Cheese Salad

Serves 2

Ingredients
4 large handfuls of kale
a sprinkle of goat's cheese
a sprinkle of sunflower and pumpkin seeds
½ avocado
2 red radishes, thinly sliced
sea salt and freshly ground black pepper, to taste
juice of ½ lemon
2 tablespoons olive oil

Method
Put the kale, goat's cheese, seeds, avocado and radishes in a bowl and mix. Season to taste, then dress with the lemon juice and olive oil.

Pea, Prawn and Tarragon Salad

Serves 4

Ingredients
250g cooked prawns
250g peas, cooked
4 spring onions, finely chopped
1 baby gem lettuce, shredded finely
a small bunch of tarragon, finely chopped
a small bunch of mint, finely chopped

For the dressing
2 tablespoons extra virgin olive oil
1 teaspoon white wine or tarragon vinegar
1 teaspoon Dijon mustard
sea salt and freshly ground black pepper

Method
1. In a large salad bowl, toss together the prawns, peas, spring onions, lettuce and herbs.

2. For the dressing, whisk the remaining ingredients and pour over the salad.

3. Toss the salad again before serving.

*top tip
Prawns are a fantastic choice of protein – they're low in fat, keep you full and are super easy and versatile to cook with

*top tip
This is a fantastic meal. The ingredients in it are nourishing and energising and the garlic will protect your heart

Zoe Kravitz's
Big Bowl of Love

Serves 1

Ingredients
2 tablespoons olive oil
6 stems purple-sprouting broccoli
2 large handfuls of baby spinach
1 garlic clove, crushed
1 mackerel or trout fillet
a small dab of harissa paste
65g cooked brown rice
a handful of beansprouts

Method
1. Preheat the grill to high.

2. Heat the olive oil in a sauté pan and cook the broccoli for 2 minutes, then add the spinach and crushed garlic, stirring until it smells amazing and softens slightly.

3. Prepare the fish with either a smudge of harissa paste or a sprinkle of chilli powder and lemon juice, and grill for 2–3 minutes on each side.

4. Toss all the vegetables together in a large bowl and serve with the fish.

Delicious Beluga Salad

Serves 4

Ingredients

200g tin beluga lentils
water (enough to cover the lentils by 2½ cm)
300g small sweet tomatoes, halved
1 bay leaf
a large bunch of parsley, chopped and stalks reserved
a large bunch of coriander, chopped and stalks reserved
1 large red onion, finely chopped
½ garlic clove, finely chopped
sea salt and freshly ground black pepper
juice of 3-4 limes
splash of balsamic vinegar
½ red, green and yellow peppers, finely chopped
2 ripe avocados, diced
4 tablespoons olive oil
200g baby spinach and mixed salad leaves

Method

1. Rinse and pick out any dirt from the lentils. Place the lentils in a saucepan with the water, one third of the tomatoes, a bay leaf and the stalks from the parsley and coriander. Don't worry about how much water you put in to start with, just add more as needed. Bring to the boil, then reduce to a simmer. (You need all the water to be absorbed, so the lentils are soft, but not too wet.)

2. While the lentils are boiling (30-35 minutes), place the red onion and garlic in a bowl. Add the salt and pepper, lime juice and balsamic vinegar. Leave the onion to marinate in the liquid while the lentils are boiling.

3. When the lentils are done and seasoned, leave them to cool until they are lukewarm, then remove the bay leaf and add the lentils to the red onion and garlic.

4. Add the peppers, the chopped herbs, the remaining tomatoes and avocados, season with some olive oil, freshly ground black pepper and salt and maybe some more lime juice. The idea is to get a bit of warmth from the ground black pepper and acidity from the lime and to combine the freshness of the coriander with the buttery taste of ripe avocado.

5. Serve on a bed of mixed salad leaves and baby spinach.

*top tip

This is a great dish for vegans. Always add some (healthy) fat to your salads because it helps your body absorb the nutrients from the vegetables more efficiently. Add a drizzle of oil, some avocado or a sprinkling of nuts

Lentils, Pecan and Roast Beetroot Salad with Goat's Cheese

Serves 4

Ingredients

4 large raw beetroots, scrubbed and peeled if skin is thick
4 garlic cloves
200g puy lentils
1 red onion, finely sliced
1 tablespoon flaxseed oil
1 teaspoon Dijon mustard
1 teaspoon red wine vinegar
sea salt and freshly ground black pepper
a small bunch of parsley
100g pecans, toasted and roughly chopped
100g goat's cheese

Method

1. Preheat the oven to 200°C/400°F/gas mark 6.

2. Wrap the beetroot together with a garlic clove in foil and roast in the oven for approximately 45 minutes or until tender. Let cool and then peel and cut into small wedges.

3. Meanwhile, place the lentils in a pan and cover with cold water. Bring to the boil and simmer for approximately 15–20 minutes until cooked, but with bite. Drain and toss with the red onions and beetroots.

4. Whisk together the oil, mustard, vinegar and salt and pepper. Pour over the lentils and mix the parsley in. Add the pecans and serve topped with the goat's cheese.

Quiche with Brown Rice Crust

Serves 4

Ingredients

For the brown rice crust
270g cooked brown rice
1 organic egg white

For the filling
vegetables of your choice, e.g. broccoli, peppers, spinach
3 large organic eggs
50g Cheddar cheese, grated
175ml rice milk
herbs of your choice, e.g. basil, parsley

Method

1. Preheat the oven to 180°C/350°F/gas mark 4.

2. To make the crust, mix the ingredients by hand, then press together with the back of a spoon to make compact. Place in the preheated oven and bake for 10 minutes. Remove from the oven and turn heat up to 200°C/400°F/gas mark 6.

3. Place your chosen vegetables in base of the cooked brown rice crust.

4. Mix the remaining filling ingredients in a blender for 30 seconds, then pour over the vegetables and bake for 40 minutes.

*serving suggestion

This goes well with grilled turkey breast or any other clean and lean protein like chicken or white fish

Hugh Grant's
Cold Lamb Salad

Serves 4

4 slices cold, pre-cooked lamb
4 large tomatoes, sliced
250g mozzarella, sliced
olive oil, for drizzling
pinch of sea salt and freshly ground
black pepper

Method

Simply arrange the ingredients on a plate,
season with a twist of pepper and drizzle over
olive oil. Pour over the salad and enjoy!

When my good friend and
mentor, James Duigan told me
he was writing another bestseller,
I couldn't stop giggling with
excitement. I read his recipes
every night and I already feel
thinner. James is very handsome
Hugh Grant

Red and Yellow
Salad with Seared
Mackerel

Serves 4

Ingredients

1 yellow pepper, finely sliced
1 box cherry tomatoes, quartered
2 carrots, peeled and grated
a bunch of coriander, leaves picked
off stalks
2 tablespoon pumpkin seeds, lightly
toasted
1 tablespoon flaxseed oil
juice of ½ lemon
sea salt and freshly ground black pepper
4 mackerel fillets
olive oil, for drizzling

Method

1. Mix together the pepper, tomatoes, carrots,
coriander and pumpkin seeds, then dress
with the flaxseed oil, lemon juice and salt
and pepper.

2. Score the skin of the mackerel fillets and
season both sides with salt and pepper.

3. Heat a heavy-based frying pan and drizzle
the skin of the fish with olive oil. Sear skin-
side down first for 2–3 minutes, then flip and
repeat on the flesh side.

4. Serve the mackerel with the salad.

Green Super Salad
Serves 4

Ingredients
100g green beans, trimmed
a bunch of asparagus, trimmed
100g baby spinach
a small bunch of rocket
½ cucumber, halved, deseeded and sliced
100g frozen peas, defrosted
2 tablespoons pine nuts, lightly toasted

For the dressing
a small bunch of basil, finely chopped
a small bunch of tarragon, finely chopped
3 tablespoons extra virgin olive oil
2 teaspoons white wine vinegar
1 teaspoon Dijon mustard
sea salt and freshly ground black pepper

Method
1. Blanch the green beans and asparagus quickly in a pan of boiling salted water until tender with a little bite. Drain and run under cold water to cool and prevent them cooking any further. Cut the tips off the asparagus and set aside.

2. In a large salad bowl, toss together the spinach, rocket and cucumber. Scatter over the peas, asparagus stalks and green beans, then sprinkle over the pine nuts and the reserved asparagus tips.

3. To make the dressing, whisk together the herbs, olive oil, vinegar, mustard and salt and pepper. Pour over the salad and enjoy!

*it's easy
This will give you a fantastic hit of vitamins, which will strengthen your immune system

*top tip
Beef is a fantastic source of protein. It's a good meal to have when you're feeling run down because it boosts your energy levels

Crunchy Cambodian-Style Beef Salad

Serves 4

Ingredients
500g fillet of beef
1 teaspoon olive oil
sea salt and freshly ground black pepper

For the salad
2 celery sticks, cut into thin strips
½ cucumber peeled, deseeded and cut into thin strips
raw/green mango cut into thin strips, optional (a handful of pomegranate works well with beef too when raw/green mango is not available)
a handful of bean shoots
sea salt and freshly ground black pepper
lime juice, to taste
1 teaspoon olive oil

To serve
1 red onion, diced
a handful of crushed cashews, to serve

For the dressing
2 garlic cloves, crushed
1 red chilli
a bunch of coriander
juice of 2 limes
2 teaspoons finely chopped ginger
2 tablespoons chicken stock
sea salt and freshly ground black pepper, to taste

Method

1. Heat a griddle pan until white hot.

2. Rub the beef fillet with the olive oil and a small pinch of salt and pepper and grill until medium-rare, about 2–3 minutes on each side. Let stand while you prepare the salad.

3. In a large bowl, toss all the salad ingredients together with the salt, pepper, lime juice and olive oil. Transfer to a serving plate in a crunchy, neat mound.

4. Thinly slice the beef and lay on top of the salad mound. Top with the red onion finely and crushed cahews.

5. To make the dressing, mix the garlic and chilli to a paste then mix in the remaining ingredients. Pour over the meat and salad and serve.

*serving suggestion
Chicken is also delicious with this salad. Poach an organic breast fillet in water with a tablespoon of Chinese sherry, a sprinkle of palm sugar and a pod of star anise, then leave to cool while you prepare the salad

*it's easy

A lettuce wrap makes for a quick and easy packed lunch for work and the variety is endless!

I love the Clean & Lean approach to diet and life – it's so simple and yet so effective. Once I had James' Clean & Lean mantra in my head, I found it easy to stay in shape with the right food, supplements and lifestyle choices, although I have to say my favourite part is the yummy shakes he makes
Rosie Huntington-Whiteley

Ultimate Clean & lean Lettuce Wrap

Serves 4

Ingredients
4 leaves iceberg lettuce
4 slices roast turkey
½ cucumber, sliced
250g hummus
sprinkle of paprika

Method
Top a lettuce leaf with a slice of turkey, cucumber, hummus and paprika, then, as if it were a sandwich, wrap it up with another piece of lettuce. Repeat with the remaining ingredients.

*serving suggestion

This can be done with a variety of ingredients, such as tomatoes, avocados or peppers, as well as salmon, chicken, lamb or prawns. White cheeses, herbs, garlic, lemon juice, paprika, turmeric, oregano, all work too. Whatever you have in your fridge!

Courgette and Lamb Skewers

Serves 4

Ingredients

400g lean lamb, diced into large chunks
2 courgettes, cut into thick rounds
2 red onions, cut into quarters
2 tablespoons olive oil
1 garlic clove, crushed
sea salt and freshly ground black pepper
4 wooden skewers soaked in water for
30 minutes
a bunch of rocket
a small bunch of basil, leaves removed
from stalks
250g feta cheese
juice of 1 lemon
extra virgin olive oil, for drizzling

Method

1. Preheat the grill to high.

2. Toss the lamb pieces, courgettes and red onions in the olive oil, crushed garlic, salt and pepper. Thread on to the prepared skewers, alternating between the lamb, courgettes and red onions. Place under the preheated grill for roughly 7-10 minutes before turning and repeating. Check the lamb to ensure it's cooked to your liking.

3. Toss together the rocket, basil and feta and dress with lemon juice and olive oil and serve with the skewers.

*serving suggestion

These skewers taste great on the barbecue, which adds a lovely chargrilled flavour and avoids the need for other seasoning and condiments

Chicken Skewers

Serves 4

Ingredients

4 chicken breasts, cut into chunks
juice of 2 lemons
1 lemongrass stick, broken into pieces
1 red chilli, chopped
a bunch of coriander (optional), chopped
20 cherry tomatoes
sea salt and freshly ground black pepper,
to taste
4 coconut leaves or parchment paper
4 wooden skewers, soaked for 30 minutes

Method

1. Preheat the oven to 200°C/400°F/gas mark 6.

2. Place the chicken, lemon juice, lemongrass, chilli and coriander, if using, in a bowl and mix well. Cover and leave in the fridge to infuse for 30 minutes-2 hours.

3. Thread the chicken and the tomatoes on to the skewers, evenly distributed between them.

4. Place the skewers on the parchment paper or coconut leaves and make into little parcels – folding the leaves around and tying with kitchen string. Place on a baking tray and cook in the preheated oven for 16-20 minutes.

5. Serve with a fresh green salad and some guacamole (see recipe on p. 57).

QUICK TIPS FOR LUNCHES ON THE GO

You won't always have time to make your lunch, especially if you work in an office. So here are my tips for lunches to go.

If you go to a sandwich bar...

✳ Go for a wrap instead of bread – it contains fewer carbohydrates than two slices of bread and will leave you less bloated.

✳ Get it with as much protein as possible – tuna, chicken, lamb, etc., and ask for extra, if necessary. Most places will give you a tiny sliver of chicken which won't keep you full and will cause you to snack.

✳ Don't drink your calories. Just stick to water and avoid fizzy drinks or juice, which are full of sugars. And don't drink during your lunch; instead, make sure you're hydrated by sipping water throughout the morning.

If you make your own lunch...

✳ Take in cold cuts. Even in winter, you don't need a hot lunch, so change your mindset on that one. I always have cold cuts at work – they're super healthy, super easy to make and they don't require any preparation. I love salmon, but you could also try chicken, beef, prawns or even a couple of hard-boiled eggs.

✳ Have your cold cuts with salad or some pre-cooked vegetables (don't overcook so they retain some crunch).

✳ Think outside the box. Forget what you think a proper lunch 'should' be and just take a selection of healthy foods to eat. For example, if all you have in your cupboards are oatcakes, some nuts, an apple and a cold cut, have those for your lunch. It will fill you up, takes no time and will keep you nice and slim.

If you go to a pizza restaurant...

✳ This is a tough one, so all I can say here is to aim for damage limitation. If you go to a place that serves pasta as well, opt for this with a meatball topping or, even better, grilled fish with a side salad.

✳ If you must have pizza, ask for extra protein (chicken or prawns) and order a side salad or some vegetables as well.

If you go to a salad bar

✳ Load up on brightly coloured vegetables as the reds, oranges and yellows are a result of the nutrients in them. An orange pepper, for example, is a sign of vitamin A.

✳ Avoid cheese, croutons, raisins, pasta and creamy dressings.

✳ Add good fat to your salad, with avocado, olive oil (the best dressing to go for at a salad bar) or oily fish, like salmon.

If you go for sushi...

✳ This is a really easy one – go for sashimi (raw fish) and edamame beans and salad.

✳ Avoid dishes with rice, where possible. Sushi restaurants often use rice wine and sugar to bind their rice.

*remember

You should have a palm-sized amount of protein with your lunch. Any less and you'll be hungry in the afternoon

CLEAN & LEAN OILS

* Extra virgin olive oil
* Macadamia nut oil
* Avocado oil
* Coconut oil
* Sesame oil

CLEAN & LEAN NUTS AND SEEDS

* Almonds
* Pecans
* Walnuts
* Brazil nuts
* Pistachios
* Macadamia nuts
* Cashews
* Chestnuts
* Peanuts
* Sunflower seeds
* Sesame seeds
* Pumpkin seeds
* Linseeds (ground only)

WHY WE LOVE COCONUT OIL

The health benefits of coconut oil are phenomenal and it's fast becoming a superfood thanks to its A-list following (models swear by it!). Here's why you need to go out and buy some this week...It helps with weight loss, it can ease digestive problems such as bloating, strengthen your immunity and keep your cholesterol levels healthy, and it also makes your hair shiny and your skin glow.

Many models include coconut oil in their diet because it helps the body to metabolise fat, meaning you burn more calories. You can cook with it (it's one of the few oils that retains its health benefits when heated, unlike olive oil), drizzle it cold on salad, have a teaspoon of it in a herbal tea or pour it over just about anything, from poached eggs to grilled vegetables. I would suggest you have around 4 teaspoons a day. It tastes absolutely delicious – very nutty and fresh – and you can buy it in most good health stores and some supermarkets.

You can apply coconut oil directly onto your skin as it will be absorbed and can soothe dry skin conditions. You can also apply it directly on the hair. Use it like a hair mask, leaving for a few minutes to soak in, and then rinse.

FOODS TO AVOID

* Tinned foods (with added sugar + preservatives)
* White bread, pasta and rice
* Processed meats
* Breakfast cereals
* Frozen ready meals
* Frozen chips, wedges, etc.
* Packets of dried pasta
* Packaged cakes, biscuits, muffins
* Chocolate, sweets and crisps

'BAD, BETTER & BEST' LUNCH GUIDE:

BAD	BETTER	BEST
Bad: Cheese burger **Why?** Non-organic meat is loaded with hormones and the bun is full of sugar and salt	**Better:** Burger (no bun) with salad **Why?** Make sure the salad is colourful, so full of antioxidants, and add avocado for some healthy fats	**Best:** Clean & Lean lettuce wrap with lean meat or cheese **Why?** The superhero of quick, easy lunches – a perfect balance of protein, carbs and good fat
Bad: Shop-bought white bread club sandwich **Why?** Full of unhealthy fats, processed meats and salt	**Better:** Rye bread sandwich with mustard and protein **Why?** Mustard helps speed up your metabolism	**Best:** Ditch the bread – just eat the sandwich filling **Why?** Choose fillings like chicken, turkey, beef and tuna and serve with heaps of nutritious, colourful salad
Bad: Sushi rolls with white rice **Why?** Contains very little of nutritional value	**Better:** Sushi rolls with brown rice **Why?** Brown rice has more fibre then white rice and is great for digestion	**Best** Sashimi with seaweed salad **Why?** Seaweed is a powerful antioxidant and helps rid the body of toxins
Bad: Caesar salad **Why?** Most salad dressings are full of unhealthy fats and packed with sugar and salt	**Better:** Caesar salad with grilled chicken but no croutons, and a splash of lemon juice and olive oil **Why?** Salads dressed like this are much healthier and the protein keeps you feel fuller for longer	**Best:** Clean & Lean super salad **Why?** A salad with organic protein, seeds and nuts is the perfect lunch
Bad: Fish and chips **Why?** Fried foods are loaded with unhealthy trans -fats	**Better:** Fried fish with no batter and side salad **Why?** By removing the batter you reduce the amount of harmful fats and carbs	**Best:** Grilled fish with salad **Why?** Grilling is a much healthier cooking method than pan-frying. This is one of the healthiest meals there is and excellent for banishing cellulite
Bad: Deep-fried sweet and sour Chinese takeaway **Why?** The poorest quality protein you can get, plus coated in sugar and full of bad trans fats	**Better:** Beef stir-fry with boiled rice **Why?** A good combination of vegetables and protein, but choose brown rice for added health benefits	**Best:** Chicken stir-fry with green vegetables **Why?** The perfect high-nutrient, low-calorie meal

CHAPTER 5

CLEAN AND LEAN DINNERS

THIS CHAPTER WILL REVEAL:

1. HOW TO MAKE DELICIOUS AND HEALTHY DINNERS

2. THE IMPORTANCE OF A GOOD EVENING MEAL

3. THE PERFECT MEAL FOR BETTER SLEEP

One of my favourite times to eat is in the evening. I have more time than at breakfast or lunch, so I can spend longer preparing and enjoying my meal and I love to sit with Christiane and process my day. Your evening meal shouldn't be rushed or stressful – it should be a part of your wind-down towards sleep so keep it relaxed, informal and happy.

THE IMPORTANCE OF A GOOD DINNER

Dinner can be a lot of people's downfall. You may be full of good intentions at the start of the day and have a healthy breakfast, followed by sensible snacks and a good lunch. But come dinnertime, you're likely to be tired from work and in a hurry to eat something quickly before crashing out in front of the TV and then going to bed.

That's why many of us eat carb-heavy, easy-to-make dinners such as pasta or takeaway pizza. But spend a little time on your dinner and your body will thank you for it. You don't have to spend hours in the kitchen after a hard day at work, but just make sure you always have the following in your kitchen – some clean and lean protein (in the form of chicken, fish, prawns, steak etc), lots of herbs and spices (they add flavour to your food and have plenty of health benefits) and a huge mix of vegetables. All of the meals in this chapter are a variation on these three things.

How to ensure a good night's sleep

At dinner time, try to avoid tea, coffee and chocolate. All contain caffeine and will disrupt your sleep. Your breakfast and lunch should rev up your energy levels to get you through the day, but the evenings are a time to wind your body down and prepare it for a good night's sleep. Remember, the better you sleep, the better your metabolism will work and the better you'll look.

THE CLEAN & LEAN EVENING RULES

Here are my dinner rules:

1 When it comes to your evening meal, include some clean and lean protein (such as fish, steak, chicken, turkey or eggs) and some vegetables. Please don't have a carbohydrate-only dinner, like pasta or pizza, because it will leave you feeling bloated and uncomfortable and make it harder for you to fall asleep.

2 Don't eat anything too rich, heavy or spicy too close to bedtime. It's a myth that eating late at night will make you fat (eating the wrong thing at any time of day will make you fat), but it may disrupt your sleep. There's a strong link between good sleep and weight loss... if you don't get enough sleep, hormonal changes take place that make you hungrier (especially for sugar) and your metabolism won't work as efficiently.

3 Relax before bed. The lead up to bedtime isn't a time for work, stress, excessive TV or laptop use, or any other things that cause you to become wound up and anxious. Instead, read a good book, take a bath (pour in some relaxing oil, like lavender, or some Epsom salts to help your body shed toxins), have a calming herbal tea like chamomile and try to get an early night. Remember, sleep before midnight is more restorative than sleep after midnight.

*top tip

If dinner is always a rush, have pre-cooked protein in your fridge ready for when you get home. Serve with crudités and a drizzle of olive oil and you have a meal in minutes

*top tip

This would go great with any grilled meat or oily fish. You can substitute goat's cheese for the feta if you prefer

Spinach and Vegetable Soup

Serves 4

Ingredients
1 carrot
4 asparagus spears
50g broccoli
2 large handfuls of fresh spinach
1 courgette
480ml organic chicken or vegetable stock
20ml water
2 garlic cloves
¼ onion
squeeze of lemon juice
basil or other herbs, to taste
1 x 400g tin chickpeas

Method
1. Steam the carrot, asparagus, broccoli, spinach and courgette over a pan of boiling water for 4–5 minutes.

2. Blend all the ingredients together except the chickpeas until the desired consistency is reached, then add chickpeas for 10 seconds or keep whole.

3. Transfer to a pan and heat through until the soup is just about to simmer, and serve.

Roast Squash with Feta, Pumpkin Seeds and Sprouting Broccoli

Serves 4

Ingredients
1 large acorn or butternut squash
2 tablespoons olive oil
1 teaspoon chilli flakes
1 teaspoon cumin seeds
sea salt and freshly ground black pepper
200g purple sprouting broccoli
100g pumpkin seeds, toasted
extra virgin olive oil, for drizzling
400g feta cheese

Method
1. Preheat the oven to 200°C/400°F/gas mark 6.

2. Peel and cut the squash into wedges or large chunks, then toss in the olive oil, chilli flakes, cumin seeds and salt and pepper.

3. Transfer to a roasting tin and roast in the preheated oven for approximately 35–45 minutes or until slightly golden and cooked.

4. Meanwhile, blanch the broccoli in salted boiling water for approximately 4 minutes, or until al dente. Once cooked, toss with the squash and pumpkin seeds.

5. Serve with a drizzle of extra virgin olive oil and the feta crumbled over the top.

Angus Beef Carpaccio with Rocket Salad and Parmesan Shavings

Serves 4

Ingredients

320g beef fillet
20g Parmesan
40g rocket
generous pinch of sea salt and freshly ground black pepper
100ml extra virgin olive oil
2 lemons

Method

1. Trim and cut the beef fillet into about 16 slices. Tenderise the beef fillet between plastic sheets until paper thin. Layer the thin pieces of beef on a plate in a round shape.

2. Shave the Parmesan, using a vegetable peeler to ensure nice long, thin pieces.

3. Wash and dry the rocket, season with salt and a little olive oil. Add to the carpaccio plate.

4. Squeeze the lemons into a bowl and add the extra virgin olive oil. Season and mix until smooth. Pour the dressing over the prepared carpaccio and rocket salad and top with the Parmesan shavings. Finish with sea salt and black pepper and a drizzle of extra virgin olive oil.

Chickpea and Carrot Stew

Serves 4

Ingredients

2 tablespoons olive oil, plus extra for drizzling
2 onions, chopped
2 garlic cloves, thinly sliced
1 teaspoon ground coriander
1 teaspoon ground cinnamon
1 teaspoon cumin seeds
1 teaspoon turmeric
1 teaspoon chilli flakes
1 tablespoon tomato purée
1 tablespoon sherry vinegar
800g chickpeas
3 carrots, sliced
500ml organic vegetable or chicken stock
sea salt and freshly ground black pepper
250g baby spinach
a bunch of parsley, chopped

Method

1. Heat the oil in a large pan, add the onions and garlic and cook gently, until softened.

2. Add the spices and fry them for 3 minutes.

3. Add the tomato purée and sherry vinegar and simmer for 3 minutes. Add the chickpeas and carrots, stock and salt and pepper. Bring to steady simmer and cook for 30 minutes.

4. Finally, stir in the spinach and cook for another 3 minutes until it is wilted, then serve with the parsley and olive oil on top.

*top tip

Chickpeas are a fantastic source of protein and will keep you full for hours

Grilled Chicken/ Turkey and Radicchio Salad

Serves 4

Ingredients
2 chicken or turkey breasts
2 tablespoons olive oil
sea salt and freshly ground black pepper
1 large radicchio, shredded
1 red onion, very finely sliced
a bunch of parsley, leaves separated and roughly chopped
2 tablespoons walnut oil
juice of ½ lemon
1 orange, peeled and sliced

Method
1. Preheat the grill to high.

2. Place the chicken or turkey breast on a baking tray. Rub with olive oil, salt and pepper, then grill for roughly 10 minutes on each side, until cooked. Leave to cool slightly before cutting on an angle.

3. Toss the chicken with the radicchio, red onion and parsley.

4. Dress with the walnut oil, lemon juice, salt and pepper. Scatter over the orange slices and serve.

Sprouted Bean Salad with Lemon Dressing

Serves 4

Ingredients
500g sprouted beans
1 carrot, chopped
½ yellow pepper, chopped
½ red/white cabbage, finely shredded

For the lemon dressing
juice of 1 lemon
4½ tablespoons olive oil
2 garlic cloves
sea salt and freshly ground black pepper, to taste

Method
1. Chop all the salad ingredients and put in a bowl.

2. Mix all the dressing ingredients together then drizzle over the salad and season to taste.

*top tip

Lemons are a very 'clean' fruit and help your body to eliminate toxins. So squirt some fresh lemon juice over your meals

Lemongrass and Coconut Prawns with Glass Noodles

Serves 4

Ingredients

20 tiger prawns, raw and unpeeled
2 tablespoons sesame oil
2 garlic cloves, crushed
2 lemongrass sticks, very finely chopped
5cm piece of fresh ginger, peeled
and grated
1 green chilli, finely sliced
50g creamed coconut
2 kaffir lime leaves, shredded
2 tablespoons tamari soy sauce
1 tablespoon fish sauce
250g glass rice noodles
a bunch of coriander, to garnish
1 lime, quartered, to garnish

Method

1. Rinse the tiger prawns under cold water.

2. In a wok, heat the oil and gently fry the garlic, lemongrass, ginger and chilli, until well softened. Add the creamed coconut and 120ml boiling water, and the kaffir lime leaves. The sauce should be of a thick consistency. Simmer for approximately 5 minutes; do not allow to boil.

3. Add the prawns and continue to cook until they have turned pink.

4. Add the soy sauce and fish sauce and taste. Add more of both if needed to adjust the flavour.

5. Meanwhile, cook the noodles according to the packet instructions.

6. Serve the prawns over the noodles, sprinkled with coriander and a wedge of lime on the side.

*top tip

Ginger is good for your digestive health and can help your body break down fatty foods

Try to eat fish at least two or three times a week. Studies show that it lowers your risk of heart disease, boosts your IQ and concentration and it's a fantastic source of healthy protein that keeps hunger at bay. Oily fish, such as salmon and mackerel, contain more fat and calories than white fish like cod, but they also contain more omega-3 fatty acids. These essential fats actually help your body burn fat more efficiently, plus they boost brain power. Try to vary the fish you eat each week – visit your fishmonger (most supermarkets have them) and ask them what fresh fish they have in that week. They'll also give you tips on how to cook it and the vegetables it goes best with

Whole Baked Sea Bass

Serves 4

Ingredients

2 whole sea bass, approximately 500g each (I think the smaller tastes fresher)
4 tablespoons olive oil
1 lemon
½ thumb-sized piece of fresh ginger
sea salt and freshly ground black pepper
500g steamed spinach and green beans, to serve

Method

1. Preheat the oven to 180°C/350°F/gas mark 4.

2. Clean the sea bass and rub in the oil, both inside and out. Wash and chop the lemon and ginger, then put inside the fish. Add salt and pepper.

3. Place the sea bass in an ovenproof dish and cover with foil, then bake in the preheated oven for 20-25 minutes. When ready, the skin and bones should fall off easily.

4. Serve with the greens and drizzle some olive oil over the top.

*top tip

Don't be scared to cook a whole fish. It's one of the easiest meals you can make. Just stuff it with clean and lean flavours, like herbs and lemon, and bake it in foil. Simple!

White Miso Scallops

Serves 4

Ingredients

2 carrots, sliced

200ml organic carrot juice

4 baby fennel, sliced paper thin

2 teaspoons white miso paste

5 hand-dived queen scallops – coral removed

2 tablespoons good-quality white wine vinegar, to season

1 teaspoon cumin seeds, lightly toasted

a handful of small basil leaves, to garnish

For the dressing

1 teaspoon wholegrain mustard

juice of 2 lemons

120ml fresh tomato juice

1 small Spanish onion, finely chopped

2 tablespoons extra virgin olive oil

sea salt and freshly ground black pepper

1 tablespoon snipped basil or tarragon leaves

Method

1. Place the carrots in a medium-sized saucepan along with the carrot juice. Bring to the boil, then reduce the heat to a nice, steady simmer.

2. While the carrots are cooking, prepare the dressing. Whisk together the mustard and lemon juice in a bowl, then stir in all the other ingredients, except for the herbs.

3. Place the fennel in a bowl of iced water. This will firm it up nicely.

4. When the carrots are cooked, place them in a blender along with their juice and blitz to a smooth consistency. Pass through a fine sieve and adjust the seasoning to your liking.

5. Rub the miso paste over the scallops and leave to rest for 5 minutes.

6. Heat the carrot purée in a pan on a low heat.

7. Heat a non-stick frying pan to high heat. Add a little olive oil and give it a swirl. Add the scallops to the pan and let them caramelise. Flip the scallops over and leave them to caramelise on the second side.

8. Remove the fennel from the iced water and place in a bowl. Season with a little of the white wine vinegar and sprinkle with the toasted cumin seeds.

9. Before serving, add the herbs to the dressing. Then put the warmed purée on a plate. Remove the scallops from the pan and place them on the purée. Serve with the fennel slices, drizzled with a little dressing and garnished with the basil leaves.

*top tip

Scallops are a rich source of omega 3, which can also help ease symptoms of premenstrual syndrome

Seared Sirloin with Rocket and Watercress Salad

Serves 4

Ingredients
2 sirloin steaks
2 tablespoons olive oil
sea salt and freshly ground black pepper
a bunch of rocket
a bunch of watercress
10 cherry tomatoes, halved

For the dressing
a small bunch of tarragon, finely chopped
a small bunch of basil, finely chopped
4 tablespoons extra virgin olive oil
juice of 1 lemon
1 tablespoon white wine vinegar
sea salt and freshly ground black pepper
100g Parmigiano-Reggiano

Method
1. Heat a griddle pan until very hot.

2. Rub the steaks with the olive oil and salt and pepper, and sear in the heated griddle pan for 2–3 minutes on each side for medium-rare. Leave to rest for 5–10 minutes.

3. Meanwhile, to make the dressing, whisk together the herbs, extra virgin olive oil, lemon juice, vinegar, salt and pepper.

4. Toss the leaves and tomatoes in the dressing. Slice the steaks very thinly on an angle and lay over the salad. Finally, shave over the Parmigiano-Reggiano.

Seared Wasabi and Sesame Tuna with Chilli and Green Beans

Serves 4

Ingredients
1 tablespoon wasabi paste
1 tablespoon sesame seeds
1 teaspoon olive oil
4 tuna steaks
1 tablespoon sesame oil
2 red chillies, finely sliced
1 teaspoon black onion seeds
200g green beans, trimmed and blanched
1 tablespoon oyster sauce
1 lime, cut into wedges, to serve

Method
1. Heat a griddle pan until very hot.

2. Mix together the wasabi paste, sesame seeds and olive oil, and rub over the tuna steaks. Sear the tuna for 2–3 minutes on each side, then leave to cool.

3. In a frying pan, heat the sesame oil, add the chillies and onion seeds, toss for 2–3 minutes, then add the beans and the oyster sauce. Continue to cook for a further 5–8 minutes, then serve with the tuna and lime wedges.

*top tip

Red meat is an excellent source of iron – great for boosting energy levels – but only have it once or twice a week because it contains saturated fat

Grilled Cajun Chicken

Serves 4

Ingredients

4 x 120g skinless chicken breasts
sea salt and freshly ground black pepper
60g harissa paste
200g quinoa
1 tablespoon olive oil
250ml water
40g chives, chopped
juice of ½ lemon, to taste
1 ripe avocado, peeled and stoned

For the salsa

1 cob sweetcorn, kernels cut off the cob
2 red radishes, cut into quarters
100g red onion, finely chopped
1 spring onion, sliced
juice of 1 lime
olive oil

Method

1. Preheat the oven to 180°C/350°F/gas mark 4.

2. Season the chicken breasts, then grill, so that there are nice grill marks on the breasts. Rub the harissa paste over the surface of the chicken and place in the oven until cooked; this will take more or less 6–8 minutes. Leave to rest.

3. Toast the quinoa in a hot pan until it takes on a slight golden brown colour, then remove from the heat immediately, place in a mixing bowl, add the olive oil and boiling water just to cover, place clingfilm over the top and allow to steam. Once cooled, add the chopped chives to the cooked quinoa.

4. For the salsa, combine the corn kernels, radish, red onion, sliced spring onion, olive oil and lime juice. Season to taste.

5. Place the ripe avocado in a food-processor and blitz until smooth, adding seasoning and lemon juice to taste.

*top tip

Salmon is a good source of healthy fat, which can help your body burn fat – especially around your waist. Have it at least once a week

Green Beans with Coconut and Black Mustard Seeds, with Grilled Salmon

Serves 4

Ingredients

4 skinless salmon fillets
sea salt and freshly ground black pepper
200g trimmed green beans
1 teaspoon coconut oil
2 tablespoons black mustard seeds
2 tablespoons desiccated coconut

Method

1. Preheat the grill to hot.

2. Place the salmon fillets on a baking tray and grill for roughly 10 minutes.

3. Blanch the beans in boiling salted water for 5–6 minutes, until al dente.

4. In a deep frying pan, heat the oil and fry the mustard seeds and coconut. After several minutes, add the beans and toss until well coated. Serve with the salmon.

Poached Chicken/ Turkey with Herbed Brown Rice

Serves 4

Ingredients

4 chicken or small turkey breasts
1 litre organic vegetable stock
1 bay leaf
1 small onion
1 carrot
1 celery stick
a small bunch of parsley
a small bunch of tarragon
a small bunch of dill
3 tablespoons flaxseed oil
juice of 1 lime
sea salt and freshly ground black pepper
250g spinach
270g brown rice

Method

1. Place the chicken or turkey breasts in a pan with the vegetable stock, the bay leaf, onion, carrot and celery. Bring to a gentle simmer until cooked, approximately 15 minutes.

2. Cook the rice and then mix with the herbs, oil, lime juice, salt and pepper.

3. Steam the spinach over a pan of boiling water and serve the chicken on top of it with the rice.

*top tip

Poaching doesn't require
any oil or fat and the
result is a succulent,
tender chicken

Poached Baby Chicken

Serves 4

Ingredients

1 baby chicken (approximately 400g), giblets removed

2.5 litres organic chicken stock

1 bulb fresh garlic, cut through the centre

1 carrot, cut into 5cm pieces

1 leek, cut into 3cm pieces

6 fresh parsley stalks

1 bay leaf

3 whole white peppercorns

6 sprigs of fresh thyme

100g brussels sprouts, peeled and halved

100g organic pearl barley, rinsed

100g organic buckwheat, rinsed

2 tablespoons extra virgin olive oil, for frying

8 medium-sized shiitake mushrooms, stalks removed

2 celery sticks, cut into 5cm lozenges

50g frozen garden peas, defrosted

Method

1. Place the chicken in a pan and cover with the stock.

2. Add the garlic, carrot, leek, parsley stalks, bay leaf, peppercorns and thyme. Bring up to heat, but do not boil. Let the chicken simmer very gently for 20 minutes. Once cooked, remove the chicken from the liquid and refrigerate, reserving the stock.

3. Strain the stock through a fine sieve and return to a clean pan. Bring the stock up to a simmer. Add the brussels sprouts and boil for 4–5 minutes, then remove and refresh using cold water.

4. Add the barley and buckwheat to the stock and continue cooking.

5. Remove the chicken from the fridge, ensuring it is completely chilled. Remove the breasts leaving the bone on. Trim the bone and do the same with the legs.

6. When the barley and buckwheat are cooked, strain and reserve the stock.

7. Bring the stock to the boil and reduce down to 175ml. Season lightly, as this will be used as a sauce to garnish your dish with and to cook the celery and peas.

8. Season the chicken breasts and legs and fry off in a little extra virgin olive oil, along with the brussels sprouts. At the same time, grill the shiitake mushrooms.

9. Heat the barley and buckwheat mixture and season to taste. Heat the reserved stock and lightly poach the celery in it. When almost cooked, add the peas.

10. Place the barley and buckwheat in the centre of a serving plate, arrange the chicken pieces on top and garnish with the mushrooms, peas, celery and brussels sprouts. Serve immediately.

*top tip

Always ensure your chicken is piping hot and white (with no pink bits) throughout

Oven-poached Salmon

Serves 4

Ingredients
4 large organic salmon fillets, skinned and boned
a large bunch of dill
4 lemons, each sliced into 6
sea salt and freshly ground black pepper
extra virgin olive oil, for drizzling
asparagus, green beans or spinach, for serving

Method
1. Preheat the oven to 180°C/350°F/gas mark 4.

2. On a large sheet of baking paper, (tin foil will also work), place the salmon and lay the dill sprigs, lemon slices, salt and pepper and drizzle with olive oil. If you have any white wine open, a splash is a delicious addition.

3. Fold the paper over to make a parcel and place on a baking sheet.

4. Bake in the oven for approximately 15-20 minutes, until the fish is completely pink and flakes away.

5. Serve with steamed vegetables such as asparagus, green beans, spinach.

Lamb Steak with Mushy Peas

Serves 4

Ingredients
4 lamb steaks
2 teaspoons olive oil
6 sprigs of thyme, chopped
pinch of sea salt and freshly ground black pepper

For the mushy peas
400g peas
50g butter
4 sprigs of mint
pinch of sea salt

Method
1. Marinate the lamb steaks with the olive oil, thyme and salt and pepper for a minimum of an hour, or overnight. Then grill them under a hot grill for 3-5 minutes on each side.

2. Boil the peas in water until tender, then strain and place in a blender with the butter, mint and sea salt until it has reached a soft consistency to your liking. Serve with the grilled lamb steaks.

*top tip
Lamb contains less fat than other red meats and provides many essential nutrients

Lamb Cutlets with Chermoula Dip and Roast Courgettes

Serves 4

Ingredients
4 large courgettes
juice of 1 lemon
1 teaspoon chilli flakes
sea salt and freshly ground black pepper
2 tablespoons olive oil
2 garlic cloves, peeled and crushed
8 lamb cutlets

For the chermoula
a bunch of parsley
a bunch of coriander
a bunch of mint
zest of 1 lemon
3 anchovy fillets, in olive oil
2 tablespoons olive oil
sea salt and freshly ground black pepper
a bunch of rocket
a bunch of watercress

*top tip
You can substitute the courgettes for your favourite greens – such as beans or broccoli

Method

1. Preheat the oven to 190°C/375°F/gas mark 5.

2. Slice the courgettes in half, lengthways. Make a paste with the lemon juice, chilli flakes, salt and pepper and 1 tablespoon of the olive oil. Rub the paste over the courgettes, then roast them in the preheated oven for approximately 30 minutes or until cooked.

3. To make the chermoula, blend together the herbs, lemon zest, anchovies, olive oil and salt and pepper. Adjust the seasoning if needed.

4. Preheat the grill to high.

5. Rub the lamb cutlets with the remaining olive oil and salt and pepper and grill for approximately 3–4 minutes according to your taste.

6. Top the lamb with the chermoula and serve with the courgettes and with the rocket and watercress, lightly dressed with olive oil and the remaining lemon juice.

Turkey Burgers

Serves 4

Ingredients

400g turkey mince
juice of 2 limes
4 lemongrass sticks, chopped
sea salt and freshly ground black pepper,
to taste
spring onions, finely chopped
iceberg lettuce, to serve

Method

1. Preheat the grill to 180°C/350°F/gas mark 4.

2. Simply put all the ingredients except the iceberg lettuce into a bowl and mix together. Cover and put in the fridge to marinate/infuse for 30 minutes–1 hour.

3. Remove the burger mixture from the fridge and shape into patties. You can make these as big or as small as you like. Then place them under the grill for 6–8 minutes on each side. (Time varies depending on the size of the burgers.)

4. Tear off the whole lettuce leaves, wash them and them place on a plate in the middle of the table. Use these to wrap your burgers in.

5. Serve with oven-roasted vegetables.

Rosie's Lemon-roasted Chicken

Serves 4

Ingredients

1 medium chicken
1 lemon, cut in half and zested
3 garlic cloves
sea salt and freshly ground black pepper,
to taste
2 tablespoons olive oil
200g brown rice
275ml organic chicken or vegetable stock
300g kale, shredded
1 avocado, sliced

Method

1. Preheat the oven to 190°C/375°F/gas mark 5.

2. Stuff the chicken with the lemon and garlic cloves and season with salt and pepper. Drizzle the skin with the olive oil and season well all over.

3. Roast the chicken for approximately 1½ hours.

4. Boil the brown rice in chicken or vegetable stock and steam the kale over a pan of boiling water.

5. Serve the chicken on a plate with the kale and rice and a scattering of avocado and lemon zest.

HERE'S MY HANDY 'BAD, BETTER & BEST'

BAD	BETTER	BEST
Bad: Sweet honey granola **Why?** Even though honey isn't a processed sugar, it's still high GI, leading to quick-release glucose that won't keep you feeling full for long	**Better:** Oat muesli with cinnamon **Why?** Cinnamon is great at helping to regulate blood sugar levels and the muesli provides fibre to keep you feeling full	**Best:** Gluten-free porridge with mixed nuts and organic berries **Why?** A great blend of low GI carbohydrates, protein and healthy fats that also contains plenty of fibre and antioxidants
Bad: Croissant with butter **Why?** Highly processed and with very little protein content	**Better:** Wholegrain bagel with hazelnut butter **Why?** Hazelnut butter is a great source of vitamin E, which helps protect the skin against ageing	**Best:** Sourdough toast with sliced avocado and organic tomatoes **Why?** Avocado's high antioxidant content has been shown to benefit our health and it's yummy!
Bad: Cereal with milk, orange juice and flavoured yogurt **Why?** Highly processed and high in sodium. Full of empty calories	**Better:** Wholegrain bread with organic cashew butter **Why?** A combination of healthy fats, protein and fibre helps keep you feel full for longer	**Best:** Spelt bread with almond butter **Why?** This is an incredibly yummy, quick snack and almond butter is a great source of essential fatty acids and protein
Bad: Sticky white rice sushi **Why?** Can irritate your digestive system, causing your tummy to bloat	**Better:** Wild rice sushi **Why?** Wild rice is naturally high in folic acid, which is a beneficial vitamin during pregnancy	**Best:** Brown rice sushi with a seaweed salad **Why?** Brown rice is a great source of magnesium, which helps you sleep better
Bad: Fat-free fruit-flavoured yogurt **Why?** Full of artificial flavours and high in sugar	**Better:** Organic greek yogurt **Why?** Introduces live cultures to your digestive system, which helps maintain a flat tummy	**Best:** Organic yogurt with live cultures, organic cinnamon and a handful of pistachios **Why?** Pistachios are a good low GI protein snack and cinnamon can help regulate blood sugar levels
Bad: Vegetable curry made with white rice and sweet sauce **Why?** White rice, combined with sweet sauce can cause your blood sugar levels to rise, which makes you crave more sugar	**Better:** Vegetable curry with brown rice and cumin **Why?** Cumin can help relieve digestive disorders and is a good source of iron	**Best:** Vegetable curry made with quinoa and greek yogurt **Why?** Quinoa is an excellent source of protein for vegetarians as well as a great gluten-free choice

VEGETARIAN GUIDE:

BAD	BETTER	BEST
Bad: Tinned vegetable soup with tofu and croutons **Why?** Low protein content with highly processed ingredients and high salt content	**Better:** Homemade soup with chilled fennel and halloumi **Why?** Fennel is a natural libido booster and it's delicious	**Best:** Organic homemade vegetable soup with organic chickpeas and lentils **Why?** A clean, nutritious high-protein meal and a good source of fibre
Bad: Frozen cheese and tomato pasta bake made with tinned tomatoes **Why?** A combination of high GI carbohydrate with unhealthy fats and minimal protein content	**Better:** Wholegrain pasta with fresh tomatoes **Why?** Tomatoes contain lycopene, which is an incredible antioxidant that helps fight cancerous cell formation	**Best:** Organic tomatoes and basil with rice noodles and olive oil **Why?** Basil is a great immune system booster and rice noodles don't contain gluten
Bad: Takeaway vegetarian pizza **Why?** Highly processed ingredients that are high in sugar and salt	**Better:** Homemade wholemeal base pizza with fresh vegetables **Why?** Fresh ingredients contain a higher nutrient and mineral content	**Best:** Gluten-free pizza base with organic tomato, goat's cheese and mixed herbs **Why?** Mixed herbs have a host of antioxidants and health benefits
Bad: Peanut butter soy smoothie **Why?** Full of hydrogenated fat, which can affect your biochemistry	**Better:** Homemade smoothie made with orange juice and fruit **Why?** Much more nutrient dense foods that have a high fibre and antioxidant content	**Best:** Homemade smoothie made with rice milk, organic fruit and nuts **Why?** Rice milk is a great lactose-free alternative to cow's milk and is easy to digest and the nuts provide protein
Bad: Soy burger with bread roll and fries **Why?** High trans-fat content and full of pesticides that can be toxic	**Better:** Quorn burger in a wholegrain roll with a garden salad **Why?** A much better source of protein with a high amount of dietary fibre to help aid digestion	**Best:** Tempeh burger (no roll) with organic roasted vegetables **Why?** A great source of protein that is incredibly nutrient dense for vegetarians
Bad: Supermarket frozen cheese quiche **Why?** Highly processed and high GI – a recipe for weight gain	**Better:** Homemade shallot tart with goat's cheese **Why?** A lighter option with no artificial flavours and preservatives	**Best:** Bell peppers stuffed with mushrooms and feta cheese **Why?** Mushrooms are a good source of vitamin D

CHAPTER 6

CLEAN AND LEAN AROUND THE WORLD

THIS CHAPTER WILL REVEAL:

1. HOW OTHER COUNTRIES AND CULTURES STAY HEALTHY

2. DELICIOUS CLEAN & LEAN DISHES FROM AROUND THE WORLD

3. HOW TO COOK CLEAN & LEAN

At the very beginning of the book, I spoke about the fact I'm Australian and how this has influenced the foods I eat and the way I cook. In Australia, eating is a very sociable experience – we love getting lots of friends together and enjoying BBQs, fresh fish and seasonal vegetables. I'm lucky in that my work has taken me around the world and, along the way, I've learned about how other countries cook and eat. In this chapter, I'll be sharing with you some fantastic recipes I've picked up on my travels ...

Australia

The Australians love a BBQ, which is a very healthy way of cooking lovely, lean steaks and fresh fish because it allows any excess fat to drain away from the food before it reaches your tummy. They also love grilling and lightly stir-frying or steaming colourful vegetables.

The extensive Australian coastline means seafood – in particular crab, lobster, prawn, tuna, salmon and abalone – is readily available. They're all high in protein, with the more oily fishes packed with fat-burning and tummy-flattening essential fatty acid omega-3, which is also heart-healthy. Australian dishes often use locally grown vegetables rich in the antioxidant vitamins A and C. They typically eat seasonally, so artichokes and asparagus in spring and capsicum and courgettes in the summer.

Thailand

While Thai food has long been ranked as one of the healthiest, the Westernised version is covered in thick, gloopy and highly processed sauces. Thai food is traditionally prepared in a stir-fry style, and this speedy cooking approach means the food keeps a lot of its natural flavour and nutrients. They also steam a lot of their food, which also retains nutrients.

Thai dishes typically contain lots of fresh lean meat, fish and vegetables and rely on fresh nutrient-rich herbs and spices such as turmeric, coriander and lemongrass. These ingredients are packed full of antioxidants and help to increase energy levels, as well as promote overall health.

The Caribbean

The hot, tropical climate of the Caribbean is great for growing fresh fruit, vegetables and herbs. Caribbean dishes often contain fresh local fish, such as red snapper, mahi mahi, and blue marlin. Grilling, BBQing and steaming are popular and all are low-fat ways of cooking. In the Caribbean, fish and meats often undergo a long preparatory process in order to enhance their taste. Lean chicken, for example, is usually washed several times with water and vinegar and left overnight to marinate in a mix of fresh herbs. Natural ingredients mean that food is flavoursome without artificial flavourings and colourings. Nutmeg, cinnamon and ginger are typical flavourings found in the Caribbean.

France

French women don't stay so slim on cheese and croissants alone. In fact, the French like to keep cooking simple and use lots of fresh ingredients bought from the local markets. These natural ingredients avoid the need to use lots of artificial flavourings and additives.

While specialities differ between regions, French cuisine is centred around fresh vegetables and lots of protein. In particular, courgettes, which are low in calories and packed with vitamin C, and tomatoes which are high in vitamins C and E are a staple part of French dishes. Mussels, which are low in salt, fat and cholesterol, and fresh fish, are all high in protein and omega-3 fatty acids. Heart-healthy olives and olive oil are also popular.

Greece

The Greeks use lots of olive oil too, which is high in antioxidants. Dishes are often prepared 'mezze-style', a Greek version of the Spanish tapas, consisting of several small dishes including vine leaves, tzatziki, kalamata, olives and grilled meats.

The Greek diet is built around oils, nuts, grains, cheese and vegetables, plus they take advantage of the locally grown wild greens and herbs like oregano, parsley, thyme and basil, which are typically low in calories, full of vitamin C and rich in folic acid. Greeks have fantastic access to fresh produce, and eat a large amount of fruit and vegetables. Fresh local fish, such as halibut, red mullet, swordfish and octopus, which are high in protein and low in fat, are also an important part of the Greek diet.

Italian Baked Aubergine

Serves 4

Ingredients
2 large aubergines, halved
olive oil, for drizzling
sea salt and freshly ground black pepper
2 tablespoons olive oil
1 onion, finely chopped
2 garlic cloves, crushed
1 tablespoon tomato purée
1 tablespoon red wine vinegar
1 x 400g tin chopped tomatoes
2 tablespoons green olives, halved
1 tablespoon capers, rinsed
200g ricotta, whisked

To serve
a small bunch of basil
a bunch of rocket

Method

1. Preheat the oven to 200°C/400°F/gas mark 6.

2. Place the aubergine halves in an ovenproof dish and drizzle with olive oil, salt and pepper. Place in the preheated oven and roast for approximately 35-45 minutes, or until soft.

3. Meanwhile in a pan, heat the 2 tablespoons of olive oil and gently cook the onion and garlic, until soft. Increase the heat and add the tomato purée and cook for a further 3-4 minutes. Add the vinegar and simmer for 2 minutes. Now add the chopped tomatoes and some salt and pepper. Bring to a steady simmer and cook for 15-20 minutes. Add the olives and capers and adjust the seasoning, if needed.

4. Spoon the sauce over the aubergines and top with the ricotta. Return to the oven for another 10 minutes before serving on the rocket with basil leaves scattered over the top.

*it's easy

Homemade hummus is so easy to make and tastes way better than the shop-bought version

Hummus

Serves 4

Ingredients
250g chickpeas
3-5 tablespoons lemon juice (depending on taste)
1½ tablespoons tahini
2 garlic cloves, crushed
½ teaspoon sea salt
2 tablespoons olive oil
parsley, to garnish (optional)

Method

1. Soak the chickpeas overnight in cold water, then boil until soft, but not mashed. Drain and reserve the liquid, then leave to cool.

2. Combine the remaining ingredients in a blender or food-processor. Add 120ml of the reserved liquid from the chickpeas. Blend for 3-5 minutes on low until thoroughly mixed and smooth.

3. Transfer to a serving bowl and create a shallow well in the centre of the hummus.

4. Pour a small amount (1-2 tablespoons) of olive oil in the well and garnish with parsley (optional). Serve immediately with fresh, warm or toasted pitta bread, or cover and refrigerate.

*top tip

A recent study found that coriander can help treat the effects of food poisoning. In fact, several herbs have healing properties: Mint helps improve digestions, thyme can soothe sore throats and reduces coughs, rosemary helps boost the circulation and aids digestion, parsley, full of vitamin C and iron, can help improve immunity and cinnamon, full of health-boosting antioxidants, can keep your blood sugar levels steady, which prevents sugar cravings

Hamour Tagine

Serves 4

Ingredients
800g hamour fillets
1kg new potatoes
2 red peppers
2 green peppers
2 large tomatoes
2 lemons
30ml olive oil
green olives and pickled lemon, to garnish

For the marinade (chermoula)
1 lemon
3 garlic cloves
a bunch of parsley
a bunch of coriander
sea salt and freshly ground black pepper
1 teaspoon paprika
1 teaspoon cumin
1 teaspoon cinnamon
60ml olive oil

Method

1. Cut the hamour fillets into equal-sized slices.

2. For the chermoula, squeeze the juice from the lemon, crush the garlic cloves, chop the parsley and coriander and mix together. Season with salt and pepper and add the paprika, cumin, cinnamon and olive oil. Mix and add the fish. Leave for about 1 hour.

3. Meanwhile, peel the potatoes and cut into slices.

4. Wash the red and green peppers and cut into strips. Wash the tomatoes and slice the lemons.

5. Heat the olive oil in a saucepan and add the potatoes. Add the marinated hamour and the remaining chermoula and pour in a glass of water.

6. Add the peppers and lemon slices and simmer on a low heat for about 30 minutes. Add the tomatoes and continue to cook for 15 minutes. Arrange in a tagine dish and garnish with the green olives and zest of pickled lemon.

Persian Pomegranate Lamb Kofte with Buckwheat

Serves 4

Ingredients
400g lean minced lamb
2 garlic cloves, crushed
a bunch of coriander, leaves and roots separated and chopped
1 small red onion, finely chopped
1 green chilli, deseeded and sliced
2 tablespoons pomegranate syrup
sea salt and freshly ground black pepper
120g buckwheat
a bunch of parsley, chopped
1 small cucumber, deseeded and diced
100g pine nuts, toasted
seeds of 1 pomegranate
2 tablespoons flaxseed oil
juice of 1 lemon
natural yogurt, to serve

Method
1. In a food-processor, blend the lamb, garlic, coriander roots, red onion, chilli, pomegranate syrup and salt and pepper.

2. Once well blended, shape into small balls (should make roughly 16-20).

3. Meanwhile, soak the buckwheat in boiling water, just covering it. Leave to sit for 15-20 minutes, then fluff up with a fork.

4. Preheat the grill. Place the lamb kofte on a wire rack on a baking tray and grill for 4-5 minutes before turning and repeating.

5. Mix the buckwheat with the parsley, coriander, cucumber, pine nuts and pomegranate seeds. Dress with the oil and lemon juice and season with salt and pepper.

6. Serve the kofte on the buckwheat salad with a spoonful of natural yogurt.

Balinese Steamed Fish

Serves 4

Ingredients
a small bunch of coriander, roots on
zest of 1 lime
1 green chilli, deseeded and finely chopped
2 garlic cloves, peeled and crushed
2 kaffir lime leaves
2.5cm piece of ginger, peeled and finely chopped
2 lemongrass sticks, tough outer leaves removed, bashed and chopped finely
1 teaspoon turmeric
1 tablespoon oil, any type
sea salt and freshly ground black pepper
either 4 whole mackerel or 8 sardines, gutted and cleaned, heads on or off or
4 fillets of white fish, such as hake, red snapper, haddock
4 small banana leaves, or 1 spilt into 4, large enough to wrap around the fish
spinach or pak choi, to serve

Method
1. Preheat the oven to 180°C/350°F/gas mark 4.

2. In a food-processor, blend all the ingredients apart from the fish and banana leaves, until you have a thick paste.

3. Lay the fish in the separate banana leaves and rub the paste over the top – a thick layer is good.

4. Wrap the banana leaves around the fish to create a snug parcel and tie with string. Place on a wire rack over a roasting tin filled with hot water. Bake in the preheated oven for roughly 15 minutes, then untie the parcel to check the fish is cooked – it should be firm to touch and completely white, not translucent.

5. Serve with some spinach or pak choi.

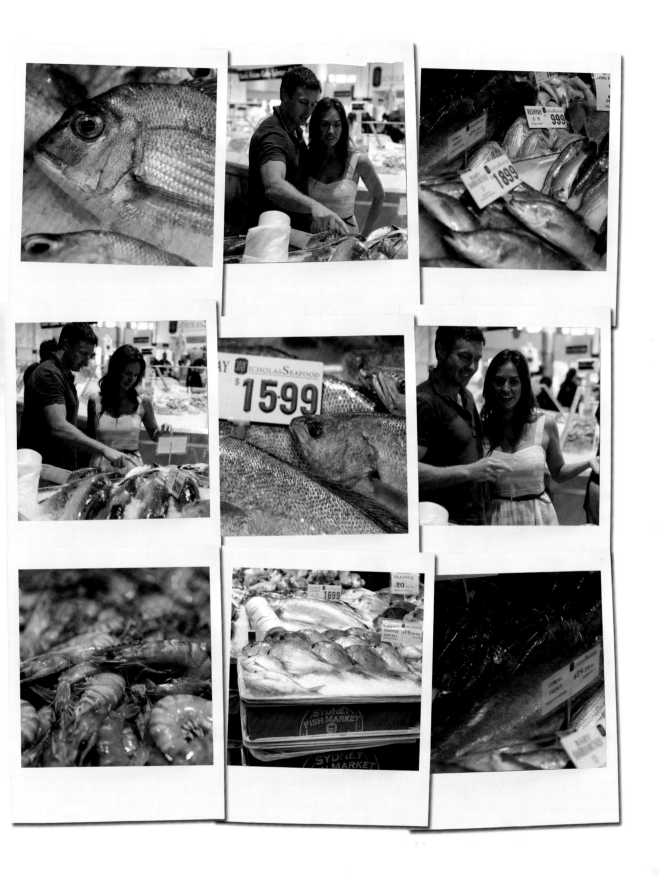

Brazilian Rice and Beans

Serves 4

Ingredients

For the rice

200g brown rice

½ onion, chopped

1 tablespoon olive oil

For the beans

400g dried black beans

1 onion, chopped

2 garlic cloves

sea salt and freshly ground black pepper

3 bay leaves

2 teaspoons Worcestershire sauce

Method

1. Rinse the rice under cold water. Heat the olive oil in a pan and brown the onion. Add the rice and 450ml water to the pan and boil. Once boiled, reduce to simmer until all the water is absorbed and the rice is cooked. (If all the water has been absorbed, but the rice is not cooked, add a little more water.)

2. Place the black beans in a pressure cooker and add water to cover with an excess of approximately 4cm. Close the cooker and bring to the boil. Once it's boiled, reduce the heat to medium-low for approximately 20-25 minutes. The beans will be cooked once they are soft, but not mushy.

3. Brown the onion and garlic with the olive oil in another pan. Pour the beans from the pressure cooker into the pan with the salt, pepper and bay leaves and leave to simmer for approximately 20 minutes. Add Worcestershire sauce to taste.

*top tip

White fish is very rich in B vitamins, which are good for increasing the metabolism and also improving your skin, cells and immune system

Quinoa with Grilled Fish

Serves 4

Ingredients

2 tablespoons coconut oil

2 stems of purple sprouting broccoli, chopped

50g green beans, chopped

½ red pepper, chopped

½ yellow pepper, chopped

200g quinoa

4 fillets sea bream

zest of 1 lemon

2.5cm piece of ginger, peeled and grated

Method

1. Preheat the grill to high.

2. Heat the coconut oil in a sauté pan over a medium heat and fry the chopped vegetables until they are cooked but retain a slight crunch.

3. Cook the quinoa in another pan with 400ml water until the water has evaporated and it's al dente. When the quinoa is ready put it in to the pan with the vegetables and mix it together. Keep warm.

4. Spread the lemon and ginger over the fish and grill for 8-10 minutes.

Salmon Sashimi with Paperthin Salad

Serves 4

Ingredients
200g skinless boneless fresh salmon fillet
freshly ground black pepper

For the paperthin salad
2 baby carrots
2 baby green courgettes
2 baby turnips
4 red radishes
2 baby beetroots
a bowlful of iced water

For the dressing
100g jalapeño chilli, deseeded and
finely chopped
½ tablespoon sea salt
1 garlic clove, chopped
80ml rice vinegar
160ml grapeseed oil

Method

1. Preheat a non-stick frying pan until medium-hot and season the salmon fillets with black pepper, then sear them for 5 seconds on each side. Make sure that all the outside has been completely seared and has turned white, then plunge them immediately into iced water to stop the cooking process. Drain and pat dry with kitchen paper, then refrigerate.

2. Prepare the salad, keeping the beetroots on the side. Slice the baby vegetables lengthways very thinly (about 1mm thick) on a mandolin grater into a bowl of iced water. Leave them in the iced water for 5 minutes to make them crunchy.

3. Repeat the same process with the beetroot, but place the slices in a separate bowl of iced water, to stop the colour from running into the other vegetables.

4. Drain the baby vegetables and the beetroot and then mix together.

5. Make up the jalapeño dressing by whisking together all the ingredients. Pour into the bottom of the serving dish, so that it completely covers the base.

6. Cut the chilled, seared salmon into slices about 5mm thick and arrange across the centre of the plate, then place the vegetable salad in the centre on top of the salmon.

Fish Papillote

Serves 4

Ingredients

4 x 200g Halwayoo fillets or monkfish
160g mussels
80g clams
juice of 1 lemon
80g unsalted butter, plus extra for cooking
1 onion, chopped
2 garlic cloves, sliced
a sprig of thyme
a small bunch of coriander
80ml fish stock
40ml white wine
sea salt and freshly ground black pepper,
to taste
200g rice, steamed

Method

1. Preheat the oven to 200°C/400°F/gas
mark 6.

2. Thinly slice the Halwayoo fillets.

3. Steam the mussels and clams in a little
lemon juice and cover until they just start
to open. Set aside.

4. Sauté the onion and garlic in a little butter
until soft. Add the herbs and then remove
from the heat.

5. Take 4 sheets of greaseproof paper and
place some onion and herbs, along with
the clams and mussels in the middle of
each sheet.

6. Lay the fish on top and pick up the edges
of the paper, so the stock and wine will not
come out. Pour in the stock, white wine and
butter, and then fold over the paper to form
a parcel, and staple shut.

7. Place on a hot oven tray and cook in the
preheated oven for 10–15 minutes. Once
done, cut open the paper and serve with
some steamed rice.

*top tip

Try to buy the freshest fish possible —
go to your local fishmonger and
ask what they have in that day

Portuguese
Salt Cod

Serves 4

Ingredients

1 large onion, thinly sliced
1 red chilli, thinly sliced
2 garlic cloves, thinly sliced
1 tablespoon olive oil
2 tablespoons tomato purée
1 teaspoon smoked paprika
2 tablespoons sherry or red wine vinegar
1 x 400g tin chopped tomatoes
1 x 400g tin cooked chickpeas
sea salt and freshly ground black pepper
400g salt cod, soaked overnight, rinsed and
drained twice
a bunch of parsley, chopped
olive oil, for drizzling

Method

1. In a large pan, gently fry the onion, chilli
and garlic in the olive oil until softened, then
add the tomato purée and paprika and fry
for a further 3 minutes. Add the vinegar and
simmer for 2–3 minutes. Add the tomatoes,
chickpeas and salt and pepper and bring to a
steady simmer.

2. Add the salt cod and continue to cook over
a gently simmer for roughly 15 minutes, until
the cod is cooked and has started to flake.

3. Taste for seasoning and stir the parsley
through.

4. Serve in pasta bowls, with a drizzle of extra
virgin olive oil and a green salad.

Cantonese Steamed Sea Bass with Shiitake Mushrooms, Leek and Ginger

Serves 4

Ingredients

4 x 100g fillets sea bass
5cm piece of ginger, thinly sliced
50g shiitake mushrooms, chopped
1 tablespoon vegetable oil
2 leeks, julienned
150ml organic chicken stock
30ml oyster sauce
30ml soy sauce
30ml sesame oil
30g baby mustard cress

Method

1. Steam the fish for 7 minutes with the sliced ginger and half of the shiitake mushrooms on top.

2. Shallow fry the ginger in very hot vegetable oil for 3–4 minutes until golden and crisp, then drain on kitchen paper.

3. After 7 minutes, add the leek and some of the deep-fried ginger and continue cooking for 3 minutes.

4. In a hot pan, reduce the chicken stock, oyster sauce, soy sauce and the rest of the shiitake mushrooms until thick. Add the sesame oil.

5. Transfer the sea bass to a plate with some baby cress on top and pour the sauce around the fish.

*top tip
Sprinkle chilli onto your food. Studies show it can speed up your metabolism

Chicken Cassoulet

Serves 4

Ingredients

2 tablespoons olive oil
2 onions, peeled, halved and sliced
6 garlic cloves, unpeeled
2 tablespoons tomato purée
2 bay leaves
100ml white wine
2 carrots, peeled and sliced into 2cm rounds
2 x 400g tins chopped tomatoes
sea salt and freshly ground black pepper
8 chicken thighs and/or drumsticks
2 x 400g tins haricot beans
a small bunch of parsley, finely chopped

Method

1. Preheat the oven to 180°C/350°F/gas mark 4.

2. Heat the olive oil in a large sauté pan and fry the onions and garlic over a low heat.

3. After 7 minutes, add the tomato purée and bay leaves and cook for 5 minutes, then add the wine and simmer to reduce a little.

4. Add the carrots and tinned tomatoes and a pinch of salt and pepper. Bring to a simmer and turn off the heat.

5. Place the chicken and haricot beans in a large ovenproof casserole dish and pour the tomato sauce over the top. Bake in the oven for 1–1½ hours until the chicken is falling off the bone.

6. Scatter the parsley over the top and enjoy with a green salad.

Thai Prawn and Coconut Broth

Serves 4

Ingredients
1 tablespoon vegetable oil
a bunch of spring onions, finely sliced
1 green chilli, finely sliced
1 medium piece of fresh ginger, peeled and grated
1 tablespoon red Thai curry paste
4 kaffir lime leaves
1 x 250g block creamed coconut
1 litre organic vegetable stock/bouillon
4 tablespoons tamari soy sauce
4 tablespoons fish sauce
100g beansprouts
2 heads pak choi, chopped
200g cooked tiger prawns
200g cooked rice noodles

To garnish
a bunch of coriander, chopped
1 lime, quartered

Method
1. In a large, deep pan, heat the oil and gently fry the spring onions, chilli and ginger.

2. Once softened, add the curry paste and lime leaves. After a couple of minutes, add the coconut and stock. Bring to a simmer and add the soy sauce and fish sauce. Add the beansprouts and pak choi and prawns and continue to simmer for another 8-10 minutes.

3. Divide the rice noodles between 4 soup bowls and ladle over the broth. Garnish with the chopped coriander and lime wedges.

Sesame Salmon Tataki

Serves 4

Ingredients
300g fresh salmon fillets
2 tablespoons olive oil
a pinch of sea salt
50g white sesame seeds, toasted
150g carrots, julienned
½ cucumber, julienned
5 white radishes, thinly sliced
5 red radishes, thinly sliced
20g seaweed (nori sheet)
finely grated zest of 1 lime
a small bunch of coriander, chopped
sea salt and freshly ground black pepper, to taste

For the ponzu jalapeño dressing
30g jalapeño chillies, deseeded and chopped
1 teaspoon sea salt
2 teaspoons garlic, chopped
200ml rice vinegar
240ml grapeseed oil

Method
1. Place a non-stick pan over a medium heat and add 2 tablespoons oil. Season the salmon with salt and crust with sesame seeds. When the oil is hot, sear the salmon sesame side down and cook for 4-8 minutes. Remove the salmon from the pan, set aside and slice on an angle.

2. To make the dressing, mix all the ingredients together in a small bowl.

3. Divide the carrots, cucumber, radish and seaweed between 4 plates. Top with the sliced salmon, sprinkle with the lime zest and coriander, season to taste and serve with ponzu jalapeño dressing.

*top tip

Be adventurous with fish! Head to your local fishmonger and try out ones you've never had before. Don't get stuck in a 'cod or salmon' rut!

Grouper Ceviche

Serves 4

Ingredients

4 x 150g grouper fillets
juice of ½ grapefruit
juice of 4 limes
¼ teaspoon chopped Scotch Bonnet chilli
1 teaspoon sea salt
175g red pepper, diced
110g red onions, diced
175g tomatoes, diced
50g coriander
1½ tablespoons olive oil
50g finely diced black olives
a large bunch of coriander, leaves picked and chopped
25g spring onions, white parts only, chopped
2 avocados, halved
lemon, cut into segments, to serve
a pinch of sumac, for dusting

Method

1. Cut the grouper into 4mm thick bite-sized pieces.

2. In a bowl, combine the grapefruit juice, lime juice and Scotch bonnet. Add the fish and marinate, covered, for about 10 minutes.

3. Drain the fish in a strainer and discard the marinade. While the fish is still in the strainer, salt it evenly. Transfer the fish to a bowl, add the remaining ingredients and stir well.

4. Place the avocado in the centre of the plate with the ceviche on top. Serve with lemon segments and finish with a dusting of sumac.

Fish Tacos

Serves 4

Ingredients

1 large jicama or turnip (for 12 Taco- shaped slices and 100g for the sauce)
150g low-fat natural yogurt
11g serrano chilli (stem and seeds removed)
a small bunch of coriander, leaves picked and chopped
1 teaspoon sea salt
40ml lime juice
60g red onion, thinly sliced
20ml extra virgin olive oil
12 x 60g Cabrilla fillet strips, skin off (or use haddock, cod or pollock)
1 lime, cut into wedges, to serve

Method

1. Peel the jicama and slice thinly into taco shapes. Reserve 100g jicama scraps for the yogurt sauce.

2. Purée the yogurt, serrano chilli, coriander leaves and jicama scraps to a smooth sauce and season with the salt.

3. In a small pan, bring the lime juice to the boil and cook the red onion until glazed.

4. Season the fish and grill under a hot grill for 3–4 minutes on each side.

5. Place the fish on the jicama tacos and drizzle with olive oil. Add the red onion slices, the fish strips and the spicy coriander yogurt. Serve, garnished with lime wedges.

Kashmiri Chicken and Yogurt Curry

Serves 4

Ingredients

8 deboned and skinless chicken thighs, cut into thick strips
1 tablespoon olive oil
1 large onion, thinly sliced
1 large piece of fresh ginger, peeled and grated
2 garlic cloves, finely chopped
1 green chilli, thinly sliced
a bunch of coriander, roots and leaves separated and finely chopped
1 teaspoon ground coriander
1 teaspoon ground cardamon
1 teaspoon turmeric
100g flaked almonds
100ml organic chicken stock
250ml natural yogurt
sea salt and freshly ground black pepper
200g brown rice, cooked

Method

1. In a large, heavy-based pan, heat the oil and quickly brown the chicken. Transfer to a plate and set aside.

2. Add the onion, garlic, ginger, chilli and coriander roots to the pan and cook for approximately 10 minutes, until softened. Add the spices and cook for another 5 minutes, stirring frequently. Add the flaked almonds and then the chicken. Stir well and add the stock and yogurt, salt and pepper. Cook over a medium heat, at a gentle simmer for 35-45 minutes.

3. Taste for seasoning before serving with brown rice and the coriander leaves sprinkled over the top.

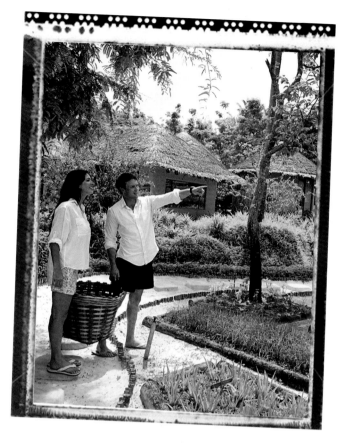

*top tip

Try this with other meats, such as lamb or beef, or fish. It tastes fantastic with prawns. Remember to vary your cooking times according to the type of protein you use

French Niçoise Salad

Serves 4

Ingredients
200g green beans
150g mixed green lettuce leaves
4 cooked artichoke hearts, halved
4 plum tomatoes, cut into wedges
100g black pitted olives
200g fresh tuna, cooked and flaked

For the dressing
2 teaspoons Dijon mustard
100ml olive oil
1 garlic clove, crushed
2 teaspoons balsamic vinegar

Method
1. Steam the green beans. Mix all the remaining salad ingredients together in a bowl. Mix all the dressing ingredients together in a separate bowl. Then drizzle the dressing over the salad and serve.

Mexican Black Bean Chilli

Serves 4

Ingredients
1 tablespoon olive oil
1 red onion, chopped
1 garlic clove, finely chopped
1 red chilli, thinly sliced
1 teaspoon chilli powder
1 teaspoon ground cumin
1 teaspoon paprika
2 tablespoons tomato purée
1 carrot, sliced
1 red, yellow or orange pepper, cut into strips
1 x 400g tin black or kidney beans
1 x 400g chopped tomatoes
sea salt and freshly ground black pepper

To serve
1 lime, quartered
natural yogurt
a small bunch of coriander, finely chopped
jalapeño peppers, chopped, to garnish

Method
1. In a large pan, heat the oil and gently fry the onion, garlic and chilli for about 10 minutes. Once they are softened, add the spices and cook for 5 minutes. Add the tomato purée, cook for 3-4 minutes.

2. Add the carrot, pepper, beans, chopped tomatoes and salt and pepper and simmer over a medium heat for 30 minutes.

3. Serve with a lime wedges, a spoonful of yogurt and the chopped coriander on top. Garnish with the jalapeno peppers.

*it's easy
When you make a salad, make a big batch and have it for lunch the next day in a lettuce wrap

Conch Salad

Serves 5

Ingredients

450g fresh conch meat (or crab or prawns)

1 large onion

1½ green peppers

3 celery sticks

1 cucumber

4 tomatoes

1 tablespoon vinegar

2 tablespoons olive oil

juice of 2 lemons

juice of 2 oranges

½ teaspoon sea salt

¼ teaspoon freshly ground black pepper

Method

1. Chop the conch and vegetables into 1–2cm pieces and combine with the vinegar, olive oil and lemon and orange juice.

2. Taste and adjust the seasoning. Keep refrigerated. Conch salad always tastes better on the second day.

*top tip

Don't overcook your steak as rare or medium-rare steak is the most flavoursome and it'll satisfy your tastebuds for longer

Grilled Rye Bay Steak

Serves 4

Ingredients

4 x 180g Rye Bay steaks

1 tablespoon olive oil

2 large handfuls of rocket

20 cherry tomatoes

sea salt and freshly ground black pepper

extra virgin olive oil, for drizzling

aged balsamic vinegar, for drizzling

Method

1. Preheat a griddle pan until very hot. Season the Rye Bay steaks, rub in the olive oil and grill for 3–4 minutes per side, according to taste.

2. Wash and clean the rocket leaves and halve the cherry tomatoes. Season the rocket leaves and cherry tomatoes with salt and pepper and drizzle with olive oil.

3. When the meat is cooked, transfer to a plate, topping it with the rocket and cherry tomatoes. Drizzle some oil and aged balsamic vinegar on top of the salad.

My top steaks

I have travelled far and wide and spent years researching all of the most celebrated steak houses and the undisputed No.1 steak in the world – by a long, long way – is the wagyu sirloin steak at the **Rockpool Bar and Grill** in Sydney – the chef, Neil Perry is a genius. Then, and in no particular order as these are all as brilliant as each other, **Mastro's Steak Houses** in America, **JW's Steak House** in London (who also serve the best cheesecake in the world, for a cheat day) and **Cut** in Beverley Hills for an incredible porterhouse.

HERE'S MY HANDY 'BAD, BETTER & BEST'

BAD	BETTER	BEST
Bad: Deep-fried turkey burger with fries **Why?** Full of trans fats, which lower good cholesterol and raise bad cholesterol	**Better:** Chargrilled turkey fillet with butternut squash **Why?** No trans fats and full of vitamins and nutrients	**Best:** Turkey breast on a bed of spinach, avocado and tomatoes **Why?** A great source of clean, organic, lean protein and a perfectly balanced meal of protein, fats and carbohydrates
Bad: Lamb doner kebab with creamy garlic sauce on white pita bread **Why?** Full of flour and sugar	**Better:** Shoulder of lamb with rosemary and garlic cloves **Why?** Garlic is a great immune system booster	**Best:** Organic lamb steak with mushy peas **Why?** Organic meat is hormone-free and peas are packed with healthy fibre
Bad: Flour tortilla wrap with fried chicken and sour cream **Why?** Packed full of added salt and sugar	**Better:** Wholegrain wheat wrap with freshly diced chicken and tomato salsa **Why?** A good source of fibre, protein and nutrients	**Best:** Lettuce wrap with organic sliced chicken and freshly made guacamole **Why?** A great source of nutrients and guacamole is loaded with healthy omega fatty acids
Bad: Fish and chips with creamy tartare sauce **Why?** Full of trans fat	**Better:** Barbecued chicken breast with wild rice and tomato salsa **Why?** Full of nutrients and amino acids	**Best:** Whole baked sea bass **Why?** Sea bass is a great source of omega 3 fatty acids (a natural anti-inflammatory)
Bad: Battered non-organic chicken in a white bun with bbq sauce **Why?** A salt, sugar and flour cocktail	**Better:** Barbecued chicken breast with wild rice and tomato salsa **Why?** Full of nutrients and amino acids, plus wild rice is a slower releasing carbohydrate	**Best:** Grilled organic chicken and radicchio salad **Why?** A light, clean, organic meal and packed with antioxidants as radicchio is a healthy superfood
Bad: Non-organic, frozen, breadcrumbed burger with deep-fried potato wedges **Why?** Breadcrumbs can be inflammatory to your digestive system	**Better:** Homemade minced beef patty with fresh cut potato chips **Why?** Homemade beef patties can be made minus the breadcrumbs and salt, which is better for your health	**Best:** Grass-fed, organic beef patties with sautéed mushrooms and sweet potato **Why?** A source of iron and carnitine, which is great for increasing energy levels

WORLD CUISINE GUIDE:

BAD	BETTER	BEST
Bad: Pasta with creamy sauce **Why?** No protein or fibre content	**Better:** Wholegrain pasta with prawns **Why?** Contains fibre and protein to help keep you feeling full	**Best:** White miso scallops **Why?** A yummy, meaty fish. Full of essential fatty acids
Bad: Tuna sushi rolls with almost no tuna, mostly rice and mayonnaise **Why?** Very low nutrient content	**Better:** Tuna sushi rolls made with brown rice **Why?** A great balance of fats, protein and carbohydrates	**Best:** Tuna sashimi with a seaweed salad **Why?** Seaweed has cancer-protecting properties
Bad: Packet seafood paella **Why?** Loaded with salt	**Better:** Homemade seafood paella with brown rice **Why?** Full of essential fatty acids	**Best:** Rock Oysters **Why?** A rich source of zinc
Bad: Deep-fried calamari with ketchup **Why?** Very high in trans fats	**Better:** Grilled calamari with tartar sauce **Why?** Squid boosts your immune system and stabilises blood sugar levels	**Best:** Chargrilled squid on a bed of kale **Why?** All the benefits (see left), plus kale helps your body to detoxify
Bad: Greasy fried lamb in a white bread roll **Why?** Fatty and full of flour	**Better:** Shredded lamb on a spit with hummus and rice **Why?** Full of flavour and without the flour	**Best:** Grilled lamb cutlets with chermoula dip and roasted vegetables **Why?** A good balance of fibre and protein to keep you feeling full
Bad: Fish pie with a lot of crust and mashed potato **Why?** Full of flour	**Better:** Salmon fillet in a tomato and basil sauce **Why?** Tomatoes have excellent anti-inflammatory properties	**Best:** Oven-poached organic salmon **Why?** Full of omega-3 fatty acids
Bad: Prawn tempura with rice and sweet and sour sauce **Why?** High trans fat content and sugar	**Better:** Prawn pad thai with rice noodles **Why?** Rice noodles are low GI so release energy slowly	**Best:** Lemongrass and coconut prawns with glass noodles **Why?** A balance of fats, protein and carbohydrates

CHAPTER 7

CLEAN AND LEAN CHEATS AND TREATS

THIS CHAPTER WILL REVEAL:

1. THE BODY BENEFITS OF CHOCOLATE CAKE (YES, REALLY!)

2. WHY YOUR BODY NEEDS A TREAT

3. MY FAVOURITE CHEAT MEALS

In my first book, *The Clean & Lean Diet*, I introduced readers to the concept of a 'cheat meal'. Basically, it can be whatever you want it to be – chocolate, a plate of ribs, some creamy pasta, fudge, ice cream ... anything – and I tell all my clients to have one a week.

The idea behind the cheat meal is that your metabolism gets such a shock from the huge and unexpected amount of calories and fat, it revs up a notch and becomes even better at burning fat. Of course, if you eat cheat meals all the time, this doesn't happen because it isn't a shock to your metabolism.

The second benefit of having a cheat meal is that it stops you becoming bored. If you eat Clean & Lean 90 per cent of the time, having the odd treat keeps things fun and stops you craving the bad stuff.

So this chapter is made up of all my favourite cheat meals, including my wedding cake.

QUICK TIPS FOR A CHEAT MEAL

Here is my cheat meal advice:

Choose your treat wisely...

✳ Don't go for something pre-packaged, stuffed full of additives and that tastes bland. If you're going to treat yourself, have something delicious. As a rule, homemade cakes, cookies and brownies taste better than packaged ones full of preservatives. The same goes for other meals – pasta with a rich, homemade creamy dressing tastes far better than a ready meal. If you're going to be bad, make it good!

Say goodbye to guilt...

✳ When you do have it, have it guilt-free. A cheat meal is pointless if you stuff it down quickly while feeling bad or ashamed. So many of us grab our favourite food – like a chocolate bar – and eat it while we're walking along the road, on the bus or driving our car. But what's the point in that? You'll barely taste it after the first mouthful because you'll be in a hurry and concentrating on something else. Instead, savour your cheat meal. Sit down and eat it slowly, enjoying every mouthful.

Don't binge...

✳ In theory, it's fine to have as much as you like of your cheat meal, but don't eat so much of something it leaves you feel disgustingly full and bloated. That isn't a treat. Eat as much as you like, but stop well before your stomach starts to hurt and you feel sick.

Eat slowly...

✳ When I used to have my cheat meal, I would wolf it down. It was like I was trying to eat it all up before anybody saw me. But that isn't how a cheat meal should be eaten. Instead, you should eat it 'mindfully' and that means slowly. Chew it properly, take in the flavours, savour each bite, breathe and enjoy it.

Leave a while before bed...

✳ Don't eat a lot of sugar and/or chocolate too close to bedtime. Both sugar and chocolate – which contains caffeine – are stimulants and they can disrupt your sleep. So try to have your cheat meal well before your bedtime.

*top tip

Listen to your body... if your cheat meal leaves you feeling bloated and windy, try something else. Remember, your body is your own nutritionist and it will tell you what it can and can't handle

Our wedding was full of so many beautiful moments and memories... celebrating with the people we love, eating good food and dancing badly (at least I was dancing badly). We also had our favourite dessert in the world – Clara's peanut butter chocolate cake! It's just so good for so many reasons and it will always bring back memories of the happiest moment in my life, ever

James and Christiane's Wedding Cake (Chocolate Cake with Peanut Butter Frosting)

Serves 8-10

Ingredients
75g cocoa powder
270g plain flour
500g sugar
2 teaspoons baking soda
1 teaspoon sea salt
235ml vegetable oil
240ml sour cream
360ml water
2 teaspoons white wine vinegar
1 teaspoon vanilla extract
2 organic eggs

For the frosting
125g soft butter
275g cream cheese
650g icing sugar
150g smooth peanut butter

Method

1. Preheat the oven to 180°C/300°F/gas mark 2.

2. Mix together the cocoa, flour, sugar, baking soda and salt. Add the oil and sour cream, all the while whisking together. Gradually add the water, followed by the vinegar and vanilla extract. Finally, add the eggs.

3. Grease 2 round cake tins and divide the mixture between them. Bake in the preheated oven for 30-40 minutes. Leave to cool.

4. To make the icing, beat the butter until smooth. Add the cream cheese and beat. Gradually, sift in the icing sugar. Add the peanut butter and beat again. Ice the cooled cake with the peanut butter frosting.

Coconut Pancakes, Agave Syrup and Grapefruit

Serves 4

Ingredients

250g coconut milk

20g grapefruit juice

large pinch of grapefruit zest

a pinch of salt

20ml agave syrup, plus extra for drizzling

2 organic egg whites, beaten

125g wholemeal flour

2 tablespoons desiccated coconut

1 tablespoon coconut oil

1 grapefruit, peeled and cut into segments

120g young coconut flesh, in strips

sprig of mint, leaves removed

Method

1. Mix the coconut milk with the grapefruit juice and zest, salt and the 20ml agave syrup.

2. Beat the egg whites, then fold them into the grapefruit mixture. Slowly add the flour and the coconut.

3. Heat a frying pan over a medium heat and add the oil. Wipe the pan for excess oil with a piece of kitchen towel and pour in 1 small ladleful of batter, 2 if there's room, and cook for 3-4 minutes on each side, until the batter turns golden. Between pancakes, wipe the pan with the oiled kitchen towel.

4. Top each pancake with the grapefruit segments and the remaining dried coconut. Serve with the agave syrup drizzled over the top and decorate with mint leaves

Naughty-But-Nice Cheesecake

Serves 8

Ingredients

200g digestive biscuits

100g rolled oats

150g unsalted butter, cubed

600g cream cheese

1 vanilla pod or pure vanilla essence

150g caster sugar

zest of 1 lemon

zest of 1 orange

300ml double cream

To serve

1 punnet organic blueberries, strawberries or raspberries

sugar, to taste

Method

1. Crush the digestive biscuits. In a pan, heat the oats over a low heat until darker in colour, then add the cubed butter and the digestive crumbs to the pan. Stir until combined. Remove from the heat and spoon into a loose-bottomed tin, flatten and refrigerate for 1 hour.

2. Place the cream cheese, vanilla, sugar and lemon and orange zest in blender and mix until smooth.

3. Whisk the cream then gradually fold into the cream cheese mixture. Spoon the mixture evenly over the chilled biscuit base. Refrigerate for 1 hour.

4. Squash the berries together to make them slightly liquidy, mix in a little sugar, then pour over the top of the cheesecake and serve.

Chocolate and Raspberry Molten Pudding

Serves 4

Ingredients

200g unsalted butter
200g good-quality dark chocolate, minimum 70 per cent cocoa solids
100g sugar
4 large organic eggs, separated
200g raspberries
30g plain flour
organic natural yogurt, to serve

Method

1. Preheat the oven to 200°C/400°F/gas mark 6. Grease either 1 large round ovenproof dish or 4 individual ramekins.

2. Place the butter and chocolate in a pan, and gently heat until melted. Remove from the heat, then add the sugar. Stir well. Add the egg yolks and stir well. Mash the raspberries and stir into the chocolate mixture with the flour.

3. Whisk the egg whites until stiff peaks form and fold into the chocolate, making sure the mixture is well combined. Pour into the prepared dish or ramekins and bake in the preheated oven for 15 minutes, or until they have just a slight wobble in the middle.

4. Serve with natural yogurt.

*top tip

This is the best cupcake recipe as they're easy to make and a teensy bit healthy. You can also vary the icing flavours by adding caramel or dulce de leche instead of vanilla

The Cupcake Company's Banana Cupcake

Makes 12

Ingredients

190g plain flour
½ teaspoon baking powder
a pinch of freshly grated nutmeg
a pinch of sea salt
150g demerera sugar
125g unsalted butter, melted and slightly cooled
2 organic eggs, lightly beaten
½ teaspoon vanilla extract
60ml milk
3 large, very ripe bananas, mashed

For the icing

250g unsalted butter, softened
500g icing sugar, sifted
1 teaspoon vanilla extract
1 tablespoon milk

Method

1. Preheat the oven to 170°C/325°F/gas mark 3.

2. In a large bowl, sift together the flour, baking powder, nutmeg and salt. Stir in the sugar.

3. In a separate bowl mix together the butter, eggs, vanilla, milk and mashed bananas. Add dry ingredients and gently mix together.

4. Fill the cupcake cases three-quarters full and arrange on a baking tray. Bake for approximately 25 minutes, until the cakes spring back to the touch (or a skewer inserted comes out clean).

5. After 5 minutes turn out the cupcakes onto a wire rack and cool.

6. Mix together all the icing ingredients in a food processor until smooth. Spread over the top of the cupcakes and decorate how you like.

Vanilla Mascarpone with Toasted Coconut and Grated Chocolate and Raspberries

Serves 4

Ingredients

250g mascarpone
1 vanilla pod, halved and seeds scraped out
100g desiccated coconut, toasted until golden
200g raspberries
100g good-quality dark chocolate, minimum 70 per cent cocoa solids

Method

1. In a bowl, beat the mascarpone with the seeds from the vanilla pod. Mix in the coconut and the raspberries.

2. Divide the mixture between 4 serving bowls and grate the chocolate over the top.

Berry Blitz

Serves 6

Ingredients

1 punnet blueberries
1 punnet strawberries
1 punnet raspberries
1 punnet blackberries
250g natural yogurt
100g shaved almonds
a sprinkle of cinnamon

Method

Place all the berries in a serving bowl. Serve with a dollop of natural yogurt and a sprinkling of almonds and cinnamon on top.

*top tip

Berries are a great accompaniment to cheat meals. They taste sweet, so satisfy a sugar craving, yet they're full of vitamins and nutrients

Dark Chocolate Fondant with Green Tea Ice Cream

Serves 4

Ingredients

For the chocolate fondant
125g good-quality dark chocolate (70 per cent cocoa solids)
125g unsalted butter
50g caster sugar
2 organic eggs
2 large organic egg yolks
15g rice flour
extra rice flour, for dusting

For the green tea ice cream
100g cream
10g glucose powder
8g milk powder
5g matcha powder (green tea)
200ml milk
3 large organic egg yolks (50g)
50g caster sugar

Method

1. First make the ice cream. Combine all the ingredients except the egg yolks and sugar and bring to a gentle simmer, stirring occasionally. Whisk the egg yolks and sugar together. Add the hot green tea mixture to the egg yolks, one spoonful at a time, whisking continuously. Once all the ingredients are mixed well, strain the mixture and leave to cool before refrigerating overnight.

2. Churn the ice cream for 10 minutes, then place in the freezer.

Preheat the oven to 180°C/350°F/gas mark 4. Grease 4 ring moulds (no bigger than 8cm in diameter and 5cm in height) and dust them with flour. Cut square pieces of greaseproof paper (bigger than the rings) to place underneath.

3. Melt the chocolate and butter over a bain-marie.

4. Whisk the whole eggs, yolks and sugar to form a sabayon. Add the chocolate mixture and rice flour to the sabayon and mix until incorporated. Pour the mixture into a piping bag and fill moulds to three quarters full. Bake in the preheated oven for 10 minutes.

5. Serve the chocolate fondants hot with the green tea ice cream.

*top tip
Green tea tea bags can be used when infused to the milk mixture, but the flavour and colour will not be as intense

Pistachio and Olive Oil Cake with Apple Sorbet

Serves 8–10

Ingredients

For the cake

50g polenta

200g ground pistachios

50g plain flour

1 teaspoon baking powder

125ml olive oil

100g unsalted butter, melted and cooled

3 organic eggs

200g caster sugar

juice and zest of 1 lemon

juice of 1 orange

icing sugar, for dusting

For the apple sorbet

400g apples, quartered

150g caster sugar

50ml glucose

200ml water

30ml lemon juice

Method

1. Preheat the oven to 160°C/325°F/gas mark 3. Grease and line a 23cm cake tin.

2. Mix the polenta, ground pistachios, flour and baking powder together. Add the olive oil to the melted butter. Whisk the eggs and caster sugar together until pale, then slowly whisk in the oil and butter. Whisk in the pistachio mixture, then add the lemon juice and zest and orange juice.

3. Transfer the cake mixture to the prepared tin and bake in the preheated oven for 40 minutes. The cake should be slightly underdone in the middle, so that if you insert a skewer it will come out with a little of the mixture sticking to it; leave for 10 minutes to cool in the tin, which will finish it off.

4. To make the sorbet, place the apples in the freezer for 2 hours. Place the sugar, glucose and water in a pan and bring to the boil, stirring until the sugar has dissolved.

5. Remove the apples from the freezer and place in a liquidiser along with the syrup. Add the lemon juice, blend, then pass through a fine sieve. Transfer the mixture to an ice-cream maker.

7. Serve the cake with a scoop of sorbet – delicious!

*top tip

Go for the best-quality dark chocolate you can afford. It will contain more health-boosting antioxidants and will taste better, meaning a little bit will go a long way when it comes to satisfying a sweet craving

Raspberry and Lemon Curd Roulade

Serves 6–8

Ingredients

4 large organic free range eggs, separated
250g caster sugar
2 tablespoons flaked almonds
200ml double cream
1 jar lemon curd
1 punnet raspberries

Method

1. Preheat the oven to 180°C/350°F/gas mark 4.

2. Whisk the egg whites until they start to whiten. Slowly add the sugar, 1 tablespoon at a time until they egg whites are stiff.

3. On a baking sheet lined with baking paper, spread the egg whites with a spatula to create a ripple effect. Sprinkle with the almonds and bake for 20 minutes.

4. Whilst the meringue is cooling, whip the cream until it holds in soft peaks, stir in the lemon curd.

5. Flip the cooled meringue onto a sheet of baking paper dusted with icing sugar. Spread the cream over it and scatter the raspberries over. Roll the roulade up and serve!

*top tip

Feel free to swap the raspberries for any berry – strawberries, blueberries and blackberries also taste great in this roulade

Roast Peaches with Passionfruit Cream and Toasted Hazelnuts

Serves 6–8

Ingredients

4 peaches, cut in half
200ml double cream
4 passionfruit
4 tablespoons hazelnuts, toasted and crushed

Method

1. Preheat the oven to 180°C/350°F/gas mark 4.

2. Place the peaches in an ovenproof dish and roast for approximately 20 minutes, until they begin to soften but still retain their shape. Remove from the oven and allow to cool slightly.

3. Whip the cream until slightly thickened. Cut the passionfruit in half and scoop out the pulp and seeds. Stir the passionfruit into the cream.

4. Arrange the peaches onto a plate, spoon over the cream and scatter the hazelnuts on top.

Chocolate Cheesecake Brownies
Serves 8-10

Ingredients
185g unsalted butter, melted
25g cocoa powder, sifted
85g caster sugar
2 organic eggs
135g plain flour, sifted
285g cream cheese, softened and chopped
4½ tablespoons caster sugar
1 organic egg
150g frozen raspberries

Method
1. Preheat the oven to 160°C/325°F/gas mark 3. Line a 20cm square tin with non-stick baking paper.

2. Place the butter, cocoa, 85g sugar, eggs and flour in a bowl and mix well until smooth.

3. Spoon into the prepared tin.

4. Mix the cream cheese, 4½ tablespoons sugar and egg in a food-processor until smooth.

5. Place the frozen raspberries on top of the chocolate mixture, then pour large spoonfuls of the cheesecake on top of the chocolate mixture and swirl with a butter knife. Bake for 45-50 minutes or until set. Leave to cool in the tin before cutting into squares.

Fruit Crumble
Serves 6-8

Ingredients
For the crumble
300g oats
100g walnuts
30g Brazil nuts
65g almonds
½ teaspoon ground fennel seeds
18g desiccated coconut
2 tablespoons coconut oil
½ teaspoon cinnamon
2 tablespoons agave syrup

For the fruit
5 large organic apples, plus any other fruit you wish to add in small quantity, e.g. 2 pears
1 tablespoon coconut oil
2 tablespoons water
1 teaspoon pure vanilla extract
½ teaspoon cinnamon
2 teaspoons Manuka honey

Method
1. Preheat the oven to 180°C/350°F/gas mark 4.

2. Make the crumble by blending all the ingredients together.

3. To make the filling, chop the fruit into small chunks. Heat the oil, water and fruit in a pan until the fruit becomes soft, then add the vanilla, cinnamon and honey heat until the mixture has thickened a little.

4. Transfer to an ovenproof dish, cover with the crumble mixture and bake in the preheated oven for around 30 minutes.

*serving suggestion
Serve the crumble with some chilled full-fat natural yogurt – delicious!

The Cupcake Company's Citrus Polenta Cake (Gluten-Free)

Serves 8

Ingredients
140g ground almonds
100g polenta
1 teaspoon gluten-free baking powder
4 large organic eggs, separated
170ml grapeseed oil
170g caster sugar
grated zest of 1 orange
grated zest of 1 lemon

For the syrup
150ml orange juice
55g caster sugar

For the mascarpone cream topping
250g mascarpone
40g icing sugar, sifted
220ml double cream, whipped to soft peaks

*top tip

For some extra zing, squeeze a little fresh lemon over this just before you eat it or scatter a little lemon zest over the cake or the cream to add interesting texture

Method

1. Preheat the oven to 180°C/350°F/gas mark 4 and lightly grease a 20cm cake tin.

Mix together the ground almonds, polenta and baking powder.

2. In a separate bowl, beat the egg yolks, grapeseed oil, 150g caster sugar and orange and lemon zests until smooth. Add the dry ingredients to the egg mixture, folding gently.

3. Whisk the egg whites and the remaining caster sugar in a clean bowl until stiff peaks form and add these to the cake mixture in three additions.

4. Pour into the prepared tin and bake in the centre of the preheated oven for 30–35 minutes or until a skewer inserted in the centre of the cake comes out clean. Leave the cake to cool in the tin while you make the syrup.

5. Place the orange juice and caster sugar in a small saucepan over a low heat. Stir to dissolve the sugar, bring to the boil and boil for 1 minute. Leave to cool for 10 minutes.

6. Pierce the cake all over through to the bottom with a skewer, then drizzle the warm syrup over the cake. Leave for 10 minutes before turning out of the tin and leave to cool completely.

7. Meanwhile, make the mascarpone cream topping. Combine the mascarpone and sifted icing sugar in a small bowl, then fold in the whipped cream.

8. Serve the cake with the mascarpone cream (or you can use the cream to ice the cake).

HERE'S MY HANDY 'BAD, BETTER & BEST'

BAD	BETTER	BEST
Bad: Chocolate sponge cake packet mix **Why?** Packed full of sugar with no redeeming health benefits	**Better:** Homemade chocolate cake **Why?** At least you know exactly what is in it, and you can use organic ingredients if you prefer	**Best:** Homemade fruit cake with organic fruit **Why?** Contains both antioxidants and fibre
Bad: Black Forest sponge cake with ice cream **Why?** Full of flour and sugar	**Better:** Homemade Black Forest sponge cake with raspberries and cream **Why?** Raspberries are low GI	**Best:** A bowl of organic raspberries and blueberries with organic greek yogurt **Why?** The berries are low GI and the yogurt is a good source of calcium
Bad: Fast food milkshake **Why?** A pure sugar bomb	**Better:** Homemade milkshake with fruit **Why?** The fruit contains fibre	**Best:** Organic fruit smoothie made with organic full fat yogurt and nuts **Why?** Full of fibre and healthy fats as well as antioxidants
Bad: Ice cream sundae **Why?** Contains almost no nutrients	**Better:** Banana split with organic cream **Why?** Bananas are a good source of potassium and dietary fibre	**Best:** Slices of banana with pecans and yogurt **Why?** A balance of protein, fats and carbohydrates
Bad: Store-bought frozen apple pie **Why?** Full of sugar and flour	**Better:** Homemade apple pie with ice cream **Why?** You know exactly what is going into it and you have the option of using organic ingredients	**Best:** Homemade organic apple pie with organic cream **Why?** Cream contains less sugar than ice cream and the pectin in apples helps lower blood cholesterol
Bad: Peanut butter shortbread **Why?** Almost no nutrient content whatsoever	**Better:** Organic peanut butter chocolate cups **Why?** Organic and contains some antioxidants	**Best:** Organic nut butter with 70% cocoa chocolate **Why?** Full of healthy fats and antioxidants
Bad: Eton Mess **Why?** Full of sugar with little nutritional value	**Better:** Strawberries with cream **Why?** The fruit contains nutrients but non-organic strawberries can be heavily sprayed with pesticides	**Best:** Organic cream with raspberries and flaked almonds **Why?** Quick and easy to make and full of fibre and antioxidants

BAD	BETTER	BEST
Bad: Ice cream **Why?** Contains huge amounts of sugar. Also, many people have problems digesting dairy and this can lower the immune system and the body's ability to burn fat	**Better:** Natural organic yogurt with almonds **Why?** Contains far less sugar than ice cream and protein from the nuts helps you feel fuller for longer	**Best:** An apple and a handful of berries **Why?** Fruit is rich in antioxidants and helps detox your system
Bad: Cakes **Why?** Loaded with sugar, wheat, yeast and bad fats	**Better:** Muffins from a health food shop **Why?** Contains fibre and fewer bad fats but is probably still full of fat and sugar	**Best:** Homemade muffins **Why?** You're able to see exactly what goes in them and can use gluten-free flour (cornflour, rice flour, buckwheat or millet) and rolled oats and antioxidant-rich berries
Bad: White sugar **Why?** Very fattening and no nutritional value	**Better:** Brown sugar **Why?** Marginally higher nutritional value than white sugar, though hardly any	**Best:** Manuka honey **Why?** Full of antioxidants, plus it naturally has antibacterial, antimicrobial, antiseptic, antiviral, antioxidant, anti-inflammatory and antifungal properties
Bad: Dried apricots **Why?** High in sugar and sulphates that destroy vitamins in the foods they preserve	**Better:** Fresh apricots **Why?** Iron-rich and a good source of fibre	**Best:** Organic apricots **Why?** No risk of sulfite exposure or any other toxin
Bad: Waxed apples **Why?** The fruit may look shiny and enticing but the wax coating drags the nutrients from the fruit	**Better:** Loose apples in a bag **Why?** More nutrient-rich. Don't peel your apples as the skin contains most of the fibre	**Best:** Organic apples **Why?** Free of any nasty toxin, even if they don't look so pretty
Bad: Instant coffee **Why?** Highly processed and full of toxins that clog up your liver. Robs your body of nutrients	**Better:** Peppermint tea **Why?** Caffeine-free and an excellent digestive aid. Try and use fresh mint leaves if possible	**Best:** Hot water with a few slices of lemon and ginger **Why?** A great detox drink and a good tip for banishing cellulite

CHAPTER 8

CLEAN AND LEAN SMOOTHIES

THIS CHAPTER WILL REVEAL:

1. WHY IT'S BETTER TO BLEND

2. THE BEST FRUIT AND VEGETABLES TO USE

3. MY FAVOURITE SMOOTHIE RECIPES

I'm a HUGE fan of smoothies. Both Christiane and I love them, and have them every morning. They're a fantastic way of getting a huge hit of nutrients into your body quickly and easily. When most people think of smoothies, though, they think of all-fruit concoctions. But my smoothies aren't like this. I include all kinds of foods in mine, from green vegetables, to nuts and milk.

Every morning Christiane makes me a an amazing green smoothie, containing anything green we happen to have in our kitchen – kale, spinach, apples, limes, cucumber or celery. It's a great way to start the day and I know that whatever else happens throughout the rest of the day, I've had an amazing amounts of nutrients at the very start.

Why making your own is always healthier

There are a few things to bear in mind though when it comes to smoothies. Shop bought smoothies are mainly made of fruit, which makes them very high in sugar. Even the ones that contain vegetables usually contain more fruit – turn the bottles around and read the ingredients. I guarantee the top few ingredients are fruit. Shop bought smoothies are also pasteurised. This involves them going through a heating process – it keeps them safe as it stops them going off – but it also destroys a lot of the health-boosting nutrients found in the fruits and vegetables. So where possible, always make your own.

It's better to blend

In the last few years there has also been a move away from 'juicing' to 'blending'. When you juice ingredients, you mix them until they're a very smooth consistency. When you blend them, you leave them a little chunkier. The latter option is much healthier because digestion starts with chewing. When you drink a very smooth smoothie your body doesn't really work to digest it and over time this can make your digestive system lazy. But when you chew chunks from your smoothie your digestive system fires up and works harder to process what you're swallowing. The pulp and fibre in a chunkier smoothie is better for your system. So in a nutshell, try to make your 'smoothies' a little less smooth and a little more chunky.

Lastly, don't treat a smoothie as a 'drink'. It isn't – it's either a meal (say, in the case of breakfast, if it contains nuts and other ingredients that make it calorific enough for breakfast) or a snack. If you treat it as a drink – especially a mainly fruit-based smoothie – you'll take in a lot of calories on top of your meals without realising.

Supercharge your smoothie:

✳ Add a handful of nuts to up the protein content (and taste and texture) of your smoothie. Protein keeps your metabolism fired up and it keeps you full for hours. Nuts are also a fantastic source of fibre which helps deal with bloating.
✳ Add lots of ice – avoid topping up with sugary juices and throw in some ice-cubes instead, plus it's hydrating.
✳ Add some supplements. I always add BodyBrilliance to mine (go to www.bodyism.com)
✳ Add some chopped herbs, like mint. They'll improve the flavour and add health benefits too.

The best fruit and vegetables to blend in a smoothie

FRUIT	VEGETABLES
✳ Blueberries	✳ Celery
✳ Apples	✳ Kale
✳ Pomegranates	✳ Spinach
✳ Oranges	✳ Green beans
✳ Plums	✳ Asparagus
✳ Kiwis	✳ Courgettes
✳ Mangoes	✳ Broccoli
✳ Bananas	✳ Peas
✳ Pineapples	✳ Pak choi
✳ Cranberries	✳ Beetroot
✳ Lemons	✳ Peppers
✳ Blackberries	
✳ Strawberries	
✳ Raspberries	

Detox Smoothie
Serves 1

Ingredients

1 scoop Bodyism Greens
240ml coconut water
1 teaspoon mint
1 celery stick
1 teaspoon grated ginger
2 large handfuls of spinach
½ cucumber
½ apple

Method

Blend all the ingredients together and serve immediately.

The Nourisher
Serves 1

Ingredients

½ teaspoon cinnamon
4 tablespoons blueberries
200ml Greek yogurt
1 tablespoon coconut shavings or
1 teaspoon coconut oil
ice

Method

Blend all the ingredients together and serve immediately.

Breakfast Smoothie
Serves 1

Ingredients

1 scoop Bodyism BodyBrilliance
1 scoop Bodyism UlitmateFibre
2 Brazil nuts
4 tablespoons blueberries
1 tablespoon ground flax
200ml rice milk

Method

Blend all the ingredients together and serve immediately.

*top tip

All Bodyism supplements are available at www.bodyism.com

Berry Smoothie
Serves 1

Ingredients
1 tablespoon blueberries
1 tablespoon strawberries
1 tablespoon blackberries
1 tablespoon rasberries
100ml natural yogurt
½ teaspoon cinnamon
100ml rice milk

Method
Blend all the ingredients together
and serve immediately.

Indulgent Shake
Serves 1

Ingredients
1 scoop Bodyism BodyComplete
2 drops vanilla extract
½ teaspoon cinnamon
2 Brazil nuts
2 tablespoons peanut butter

Method
Blend all the ingredients together
and serve immediately.

S&M Greens
Serves 1

Ingredients
a handful of spinach
a handful of broccoli
¼ cucumber
1 teaspoon grated ginger
1 celery
squeeze of lemon
100ml water

Method
Blend all the ingredients
together and serve
immediately.

Ultimate Complete Shake

Serves 1

Ingredients
1 scoop Bodyism BodyBrilliance
1 scoop Bodyism BodyComplete
1 scoop Bodyism UltimateFibre
1 scoop Bodyism Greens

Method
Blend all the ingredients together and serve immediately.

Superfood's Shake

Serves 4

Ingredients
1 banana
½ ripe avocado
1 tablespoon green spirulina powder
1 tablespoon chlorella
1 tablespoon maca powder
2 tablespoons ground flaxseed
gogi berries, optional
1 tablespoon coconut flour, optional
1 tablespoon activated chia seeds, soaked in water overnight
1 tablespoon bee pollen
6 Brazil nuts
11 teaspoons cinnamon
2–3 tablespoons protein powder
1 tablespoon unsweetened cocoa
1 tablespoon honey
240ml unsweetened almond milk
720ml filtered water
1 tablespoon Acai syrup

Method
Blend all the ingredients together and serve immediately.

Morning Booster Shake

Serves 1

Ingredients
1 glass water or milk
1 scoop BodyBrilliance
1 scoop UltimateFibre
3 Brazil nuts
a handful of sunflower seeds
a handful of pumpkin seeds
a pinch of turmeric

Method
Blend all the ingredients together and serve immediately.

Lean Physic Shake

Serves 1

Ingredients
1 scoop Bodyism BodyComplete
220ml rice milk or almond milk
1 scoop lecithin
½ scoop Bodyism Supergreens, optional

Method
Blend all the ingredients together and serve immediately.

*top tip

You don't have to stick to these ingredients – try adding your favourite clean and lean ingredients to your smoothies

Bodyism
Bloody Mary

Serves 1

Ingredients
150ml tomato juice
1 celery stick
¼ cucumber
a pinch of black pepper
ice

Method
Blend all the ingredients together
and serve immediately.

Good Night
Sleep

Serves 1

Ingredients
1 scoop BodySerenity
200ml vanilla rice milk
8 cashews

Method
Blend all the ingredients together
and serve immediately.

Anti-ageing
Smoothie

Serves 1

Ingredients
water
½ cucumber
½ avocado
1 celery stick
squeeze of lemon juice
a small handful of green leaves or
1 scoop Bodyism supergreens
1 teaspoon grated ginger

Method
Blend all the ingredients together
and serve immediately.

Super Green Smoothie

Serves 1

Ingredients
240ml water
1 scoop Bodyism Beauty Food
juice of 1 lemon or lime
5 mint leaves
2 slices of ginger

Method
Blend all the ingredients together
and serve immediately.

INDEX

MY CLIENTS

People often ask me what Elle Macpherson is really like, so I thought I'd tell you a few things about her you may not know. From the first time I met her, she has never stopped helping me. In fact, she's always looking for ways in which she can be of service to the people in her life. She's the hardest worker I know, and yet she always makes time for the people she loves. She's also very generous – in all the years I have known her she has never once asked for anything in return, ever. She always asks after my family, which is such a lovely and easy thing to do, but not something everyone does, and whenever she has anything she always looks to share it. She loves her children and she's proud of them, too, and when she talks about them she lights up. She always looks for the positive in a situation and in a person. She never gossips, complains, gives up or looks for excuses, which are all such amazing qualities. She's highly principled too. Whenever I have a new project I want her advice on, her first questions are always about its integrity. It's never about how much money she could make but whether she believes in what is being done. But perhaps the most profound impact Elle has had on my life is this. When I first met my wife, Christiane, I loved her from the moment I saw her, but it took me a while to pluck up the courage to ask her to marry me. It was a Monday when Elle walked in to the gym, She asked me how things were and how was Christiane. 'Fine,' I said. 'So when are you going to ask her to marry you?' I replied I was nervous and scared, etc, etc. Elle put her hands on my shoulders, looked me straight in the eye and said the following: 'Christiane is a beautiful person, inside and out. She will be an amazing mother and a best friend to you forever. You love her and she loves you. Ask this woman to marry you and let go of being scared.' So I did, and she said yes! And I'm so thankful every single day that I have such an amazing wife and a friend who cared enough to tell it to me straight. I'll stop there, but I hope you get the picture. She's one amazing lady.

People also ask me what Rosie Huntington-Whiteley is like in 'real life' and I can only say this. She is also one of the most remarkable, highly principled and generous people I have ever met and I'm still astonished at what an amazing and humble person she is. She's beautiful on the inside and obviously on the outside. I once asked her why she is so supportive of me and her answer was typically inspiring, brilliant and honest. She said, 'Because i believe in what you're saying and what you're trying to do. I really do support you and I want to help do something good.' I just think it's great that she has the courage of her convictions and that she constantly thinks of how she can help others. Rosie is one in a million. She's someone that I love and admire, that I can count on as a friend no matter what, which is pretty cool in my opinion. Just be careful if you ever have breakfast with her – she will eat all your granola!

People also ask me about Hugh Grant. He has become a really good friend of mine over the years and I love him very much. I just want to share a little story about him that might give you an insight in to the kind and beautiful person he is. A few years ago, one of our trainers became ill. I paid the medical bills, but it started to get really expensive and was becoming more than I could afford. Hugh knew about the situation but hadn't really said much about it other than to ask how things were going. As the months went by we all got increasingly concerned and worried. Hugh was just about to go off for a while filming but he came in to Bodyism the day he left to say goodbye. As he left, he handed me a blank cheque and said, 'Make sure she gets whatever she needs. It doesn't matter what it costs.' That's the kind of man Hugh Grant is. That's what he is like in real life and I love him for it. As he walked out he also said, 'Please don't spend it on a sex change.' Which is also why I love him. He might be angry at me for telling this story but I don't care. I want people to know what a kind hearted person he really is. (Our lovely trainer is completely healthy now by the way!)

Finally, I just want to quickly mention my amazing, wonderful and beautiful friend David de Rothschild. He has inspired me to do more and to be more. He gave me a bigger problem to tackle, to help as many people in the world as I can. Please log on to myoo.com to see how you can help too.

ACKNOWLEDGEMENTS

I'd like to **thank** the following people for making this book possible, firstly my wife, Christiane. I love you more and more every day, you were the **driving** force of this book and your **ideas** and passion are what make these things **special** and amazing. I love that you're smarter than me and I love having you on my team. You're my **best** friend and I love every bit of you in every way. Thank you for your **beautiful** heart. Elle, Rosie and Hugh, thank you for **everything**. To Zoe Kravitz, you're like a little sister to me and I love you very much, you're such a wonderful person and me and my amore miss you lots. You're kind, **generous** and special and I can't wait to see the amazing things you do in this world. Unleash your inner warrior **goddess**! To Holly Valance, I'm a better dancer than you but you're quite funny. You're also a **warm**, generous and caring **soul** and Christiane and I both think you're the best and we love spending time with you, thank you again for being so cool. To Lee for staying **awake** and helping me on that long last night before deadline, you invented some very interesting foods and your **support** is something I will never forget, I **love** you. To David de Rothschild, for inspiring me and **believing** in me and for being a big beautiful friend that gives me hugs, I love you. To Sebastian and Emily for taking such beautiful photos and being such wonderful friends. To Linda for being so incredibly **incredible**, I can't put in to words how **grateful** I am to you and how much I admire you. To Nat for being so amazing, brilliant and such a huge part of all that we do. To Clara, Megan, Michelle (and Toby and Cupcake and Bud Bud) for the **wonderful** recipes and beautiful friendship. To Dalton, for driving us home from bjj when I'm dizzy and for having the **courage** to evolve, it's amazing. To my friend Justin Alexander, OG. To my mum and dad, the best people I know and to my little sister, I'm so **proud** of you. And to Chantal and Luke and Sol, for making it all **possible** and for being such beautiful friends. We love you all so much! To my wonderful publishers, thank you Kyle and Judith and Vicki! Tommy, I literally don't know what I would do without you, **definitely** not horse riding. **Thank you** Maria.... we did it again, even better!